The
BIKE
WRITER

Insights Discovered along the
Bicycle Paths of Life

JIM BOEGLIN

 ARCHWAY
PUBLISHING

Archway Publishing books may be ordered through booksellers or by contacting:

Archway Publishing
1663 Liberty Drive
Bloomington, IN 47403
www.archwaypublishing.com
1 (888) 242-5904

Because of the dynamic nature of the Internet, any web addresses or links contained in this book may have changed since publication and may no longer be valid. The views expressed in this work are solely those of the author and do not necessarily reflect the views of the publisher, and the publisher hereby disclaims any responsibility for them.

Any people depicted in stock imagery provided by Thinkstock are models, and such images are being used for illustrative purposes only. Certain stock imagery © Thinkstock.

ISBN: 978-1-4808-4456-8 (sc)
ISBN: 978-1-4808-4457-5 (e)

Library of Congress Control Number: 2017903452

Print information available on the last page.

Archway Publishing rev. date: 3/29/2017

Dedication

This book is intended to be about life and life's lessons. During the writing, my nephew, Tim Boeglin, passed away a few days after his fifty-eighth birthday following a three-year battle with a rare form of cancer. Tim was one of those extraordinary individuals who serve as an inspiration to the rest of us. More wisdom, meaning, and kindness were packed into those fifty-eight years than most people experience if they live to be one hundred.

Tim was the third of six children born to my brother Tom and his wife, Betty. Many of his growing-up years were spent in my hometown, Ferdinand, Indiana. He graduated from the University of Notre Dame and the Indiana University Maurer School of Law in Bloomington. His one-year undergraduate experience in Innsbruck, Austria, while enrolled as a student at Notre Dame, was the beginning of an adventurous, lifelong love affair with Western Europe.

Tim and Cindy were classmates in law school and were married right after their graduation. They spent the following summer touring Europe on borrowed money before embarking on their legal careers in Chicago. Tim joined a large law firm; Cindy practiced public interest law.

Tim quickly discovered that the practice of law was not for him. After three years, he and another disillusioned attorney created their own business, XJD Corp. Tim eventually bought out his partner and moved the business to his beloved Bloomington, Indiana. XJD Corp became an innovative producer of mousepads, rapidly becoming one of the largest employers in Bloomington. Tim was recognized as entrepreneur of the year in Indiana.

Tim was an entrepreneur at heart and was the founding director of the IU Elmore Entrepreneurial Law Clinic, a joint program of the IU Kelley School of Business and the IU Law School. MBA candidates learn about the law, and law students learn about business.

Tim and Cindy raised their two sons in Bloomington and stayed closely connected with Indiana University. Cindy still teaches at the law school. Their oldest son, Gus, is a recent graduate of the IU School of Medicine, and Luke (the "renegade") is a graduate of San Diego State. Tim was the consummate family man.

Tim and I lived lives many miles apart, and I didn't get to spend a lot of time with him—mostly at family gatherings, weddings, and funerals. Every encounter with Tim was a memorable experience, and it felt to me like we searched each other out on those occasions. I am guessing that lots of family members felt the same way. Tim Boeglin was everyone's best friend.

My memory is that Tim listened with both of his ears, his eyes, and all his senses. When he talked, he was open, genuine, kind, funny, and authentic. His enthusiasm and creativity were contagious. There was not a pretentious or a mean bone in Tim's body. He was here to help others.

What if life is a journey
to a destination hazy at best?
What if each challenge encountered
is nothing more than a test?

What if hell and heaven
are located just in my mind
and I experience each one of them daily
as I choose to be fearful or kind?

Jb

In retrospect, it seems that Tim found a way to tame his ego and free up his spirit to shine through. That is the secret that most of us search for all our lives. Tim found the key early in his life experience and spent the rest of his life showing us the way.

Tim lived life fully. With front row seats for the IU basketball games, Tim's love for Indiana University can be summed up in the two words that were his favorite expression: Go Hoosiers!

The final chapter of this book is entitled "Finishing Strong." Tim was my inspiration for the chapter. Congratulations, Tim, on a life well lived. You are missed by more people than you can imagine.

Dedication

This book is intended to be about life and life's lessons. During the writing, my nephew, Tim Boeglin, passed away a few days after his fifty-eighth birthday following a three-year battle with a rare form of cancer. Tim was one of those extraordinary individuals who serve as an inspiration to the rest of us. More wisdom, meaning, and kindness were packed into those fifty-eight years than most people experience if they live to be one hundred.

Tim was the third of six children born to my brother Tom and his wife, Betty. Many of his growing-up years were spent in my hometown, Ferdinand, Indiana. He graduated from the University of Notre Dame and the Indiana University Maurer School of Law in Bloomington. His one-year undergraduate experience in Innsbruck, Austria, while enrolled as a student at Notre Dame, was the beginning of an adventurous, lifelong love affair with Western Europe.

Tim and Cindy were classmates in law school and were married right after their graduation. They spent the following summer touring Europe on borrowed money before embarking on their legal careers in Chicago. Tim joined a large law firm; Cindy practiced public interest law.

Tim quickly discovered that the practice of law was not for him. After three years, he and another disillusioned attorney created their own business, XJD Corp. Tim eventually bought out his partner and moved the business to his beloved Bloomington, Indiana. XJD Corp became an innovative producer of mousepads, rapidly becoming one of the largest employers in Bloomington. Tim was recognized as entrepreneur of the year in Indiana.

Tim was an entrepreneur at heart and was the founding director of the IU Elmore Entrepreneurial Law Clinic, a joint program of the IU Kelley School of Business and the IU Law School. MBA candidates learn about the law, and law students learn about business.

Tim and Cindy raised their two sons in Bloomington and stayed closely connected with Indiana University. Cindy still teaches at the law school. Their oldest son, Gus, is a recent graduate of the IU School of Medicine, and Luke (the "renegade") is a graduate of San Diego State. Tim was the consummate family man.

Tim and I lived lives many miles apart, and I didn't get to spend a lot of time with him—mostly at family gatherings, weddings, and funerals. Every encounter with Tim was a memorable experience, and it felt to me like we searched each other out on those occasions. I am guessing that lots of family members felt the same way. Tim Boeglin was everyone's best friend.

My memory is that Tim listened with both of his ears, his eyes, and all his senses. When he talked, he was open, genuine, kind, funny, and authentic. His enthusiasm and creativity were contagious. There was not a pretentious or a mean bone in Tim's body. He was here to help others.

Table of Contents

Acknowledgments

I extend my gratitude to family and friends who contributed to this book and made it possible. A special thanks to my wife Jan, who was not only supportive and encouraging but also did even more of the heavy lifting with our real estate business while I was focused on writing. And thanks to my two older brothers, Bob and Tom, who, along with me, are the only Boeglins of our generation still above ground. They were my fact-checkers and editors.

I thank all of the nieces and nephews who read a preliminary draft and offered their feedback and encouragement. It was much needed at the time and kept me writing.

Most of all I acknowledge my parents, Otto and Clara Boeglin, who modeled lives of service, integrity, kindness, and generosity. They have been gone for decades but are not forgotten by any of the Boeglin boys.

Introduction

I think of life as a journey of discovery—of ourselves and the world around us. We come into this world as infants who are totally dependent upon our parents and caregivers. Over time, most of us accumulate the knowledge and skills necessary to live independent lives. It is a lifelong journey, and we never stop learning.

There is an unlimited array of paths to take along this journey, and everyone navigates his or her own unique way through his or her human experience. Some of our paths are long and winding, with lots of obstacles, potholes, steep hills, and precipitous drops. Some of us find a relatively smooth path, with only gentle slopes and sweeping curves. Some have their eyes wide open; others wear blinders. Sometimes we are alone on the path; at other times we have company on the journey. There can be unexpected detours along the way. Sometimes the journey is cut short by disease or accident, as was the case with my nephew, Tim, who finished his journey after just fifty-eight years.

For many of us life is a trial-and-error process that includes multiple paths. We learn as we go—or not. Sometimes we are on the high road, moving boldly and confidently along our way; other times we are on our hands and knees, trying to dig our way out of the muck.

This is the story of some of the paths and detours I have taken in my first seven-plus decades of life, and insights gained along the way.

The Bike

The bicycle has been an important vehicle for my journey. For almost seventy years, it has been a balancing influence in my life. Since I underwent heart bypass surgery sixteen years ago, biking has also been my ongoing rehab program of choice. My cardiologist tells me it is working. In recent years, I have biked in excess of six thousand miles per year and have "biked my age" one day each year since age seventy.

But for me biking is much more than a physical workout. When I hop on my bike my "fun meter" goes up a notch. My mind seems to split into two distinct parts.

One part of my brain is aware of where I am going, traffic conditions, weather, happenings in the neighborhood, fellow bikers, walkers and joggers, safety issues, my body atop an uncomfortable seat in an awkward position, and the normal aches and pains associated with a one-hundred-and-eighty-pound body being propelled forward by legs that are almost three-quarters of a century old.

Another part of my mind is floating, thinking about such things as an appreciation of the great bike trails in our area of Southwest Florida, the beautiful beaches and parklands, landscaped neighborhoods, my personal bucket list, world affairs, politics, childhood memories, travel plans, the current state of my golf game, family members, friends, clients, pending transactions, upcoming challenges, grocery lists, religion's role in world terrorism, the stock market, scheduled appointments, future bike trips, potential blog topics, books I am reading, etc.

To be clear, I do not normally think of all of these things at one time, or even on one bike ride. Often I write down some of these thoughts and ideas either during or after the ride and preserve them in a journal. Many of my ideas for writing have come to me on a bike ride, hence the title: *The Bike Writer.*

A Brief History of the Bicycle

According to the National Bicycle History Archives of America, www.nbhaa.com, the bicycle was invented in 1817 by a German, Karl Drais, in response to a horse shortage. It seems that crop failures caused by an 1816 volcanic eruption in Europe resulted in a mass slaughter of horses, which were desperately needed for their meat. The bicycle was invented to replace the slaughtered horses.

The first bicycles (called velocipedes) were made of wood and had no pedals. They were propelled by shoving off the ground with the feet. They were not exactly high tech, compared to today's multi-geared bikes made of such exotic, lightweight materials as carbon and titanium.

In 1818 the harvest improved, and horses made a comeback as a form of transportation rather than food. The need for the bicycle quickly faded.

It wasn't until the 1890s in America that the bicycle became a common form of transportation. Pneumatic tires improved the biking experience, and bicycles became a mass-produced form of transportation for working men.

Women also began riding bikes in the 1890s, giving them more mobility than was previously available to women. Betty Bloomer's bloomers became popular, providing women with "common sense clothes" while biking. This reportedly was instrumental in bring the bustle and corset era to a close.

By the 1920s, the automobile had largely replaced the bicycle in America, and it became more of a child's toy than an adult's transportation. Schwinn and other bicycle manufacturers introduced many innovations beginning in the 1930s, including fat tires and spring forks to make bikes more durable and maneuverable.

The Gay Nineties and the Roaring Twenties were before my time. However, I remember how attitudes toward the bicycle changed again in the 1970s during OPEC's oil embargo. Americans were encouraged to use the bicycle for commuting to work to reduce gas consumption. I became a willing participant in that movement, sometimes riding from our suburban Fort Wayne home to my downtown law office in the Lincoln Tower. It was not a safe bike ride, as the route was shared with car traffic, but I somehow managed to avoid getting tangled up with motor vehicles on my commute.

The bicycle is making another comeback in the early decades of the twenty-first century, as global warming and fossil fuel consumption have become significant issues for Planet Earth. The bicycle is a clean alternative to meet our transportation needs, and many cities and towns are revising their transportation systems to encourage bike ridership.

I was recently in Seattle, and the city has developed bike lanes and bike paths and even provides bikes to entice the usage of more bikes and fewer cars on the streets. This phenomenon is going on in almost every major city in the world. Motorists are being challenged to share the road with cyclists. Clearly the bicycle has come of age.

Personal Bike History

I've been a biker since my sister, Ann, taught me to ride at age five. It has been nearly a lifelong relationship between me and my bike. I have been an active biker ever since Ann's introduction to biking.

I was born on Ann's twelfth birthday, February 2, 1943, and we had a special bond as fellow groundhogs. As a teenager, she took me with her wherever she went—I now understand at the request of our mother. I was Ann's training ground for when she later raised a family of five girls, Ruth, Chris, Carol, Mary, and Jane, and I was devastated when she abandoned me in favor of nurse's training in Louisville when I was only six years old.

I learned to ride on her girl's bike, which allowed me to reach the pedals but not the seat. My parents recognized a good thing when they saw me ride her bike, and they bought me my own twenty-four-inch bike not long after that.

From ages ten to sixteen, I delivered newspapers by bike from one end of my home town of Ferdinand, Indiana, to the other. I had about fifty customers for the *Louisville Courier Journal* six days per week, and double that on Sunday. Ferdinand has some steep hills, and I seemed to have a paper customer at the very top of every one of them.

I rode that bike wherever I needed to go, to and from church and school, rounding up players for a sand-lot baseball game, or venturing out into the countryside on my own. I lived on that bike.

Starting at age twelve, I began nagging my parents for a full-size twenty-six-inch bike to replace the smaller model that I had outgrown. Two days before Christmas that year, my dad took my bike to the local hardware store with the promise that the old bike would be tuned, repainted, and made to look like new. I was very unhappy with this decision because I really wanted a new, larger bike. When we went to pick up the "old" bike on Christmas Eve, it had miraculously grown to a full-sized twenty-six-inch version. Both the hardware store owner and my dad, with a twinkle in his eye, insisted it was the old bike but fixed up.

My dad died from colon cancer less than four years later, in 1959, never actually acknowledging to me that it was a new bike. I knew, and he knew. It was our own inside joke.

That Schwinn had a lot of miles on it when I took it with me to college at Indiana University in Bloomington in the fall of 1961. It was my sole form of transportation through my undergraduate years and a constant reminder of my dad. In retrospect, that reminder may have helped me to stay on course during the turbulent '60s at Indiana University.

I met my first wife, Donna, while playing baseball for the neighboring town of Jasper's American Legion baseball team. The Jasper High School girls often came to our games. We dated through my college/law school and her nurses training years, and married in August 1966, shortly after her graduation from St. Mary's Hospital School of Nursing in Evansville.

I was still in IU Law School when we married. Laura was born ten months after the wedding, and Mike followed eleven months later—Irish twins. Laura was not yet walking when Mike was born at 3:00 a.m., and seven hours later I was in Federal Court being admitted to the Indiana Bar Association.

When our kids were small, we biked around our neighborhood with either Laura or Mike perched in a child seat that would not meet today's safety standards. They both survived the experience. Eventually they got big enough for their own bikes, and we spent family biking vacations at such places as Mackinac Island, Cape Cod, and Jekyll Island. Mike and I made one challenging camping trip from Fort Wayne to Chain-of-Lakes State Park—about thirty-five miles each way—when he was thirteen years old.

Somewhere along the way, I passed down the story of my "miracle bike" that appeared that Christmas Eve when I was twelve. Laura and Mike never knew their grandpa, who had died years before they were born. I think they now have a sense of who he was.

Through the years, I have biked much of Michigan, Wisconsin, Ohio, Pennsylvania, Massachusetts, Maine, Maryland, Indiana, Georgia, Alabama, and Florida. Eventually we upgraded our bikes to light, multi-geared versions. About twenty years ago, my wife, Jan, and I took a memorable bike trip through Germany with our friends Dave and Sandy. We lived on our bikes for two weeks, exploring the Romantic Road from Heidelberg to Augsburg.

In 2001, I underwent triple bypass surgery at Parkview Hospital in Fort Wayne, due to clogged arteries. It was a challenging surprise to me, as I had kept physically active and fit through the years. Our family has a long history of high cholesterol, and it apparently did its number on my arteries. Within a few months following the surgery, I was back on my bike and determined to control this disease through exercise and diet. It has been an effective remedy so far.

About six years ago, my son and I biked 353 miles from Bonita Springs to Gainesville as a fundraiser for the Bonita Springs Assistance Office, which operates a food pantry for needy residents. It was ten years after my heart surgery and five years before Mike's open heart surgery to have his aortic valve replaced due to a birth defect. We were a couple of heart patients, looking after each other and making sure neither of us came under too much stress.

Friends, family, and clients pledged a total of nearly ten dollars per mile for our adventure. We blogged each night, keeping our sponsors and friends informed of our progress. It was a weeklong bonding experience that neither Mike nor I will ever forget. We raised $3,500 for the food pantry in the process. Jan picked us up near Gainesville, where we put our bikes on the car and continued north to Indiana for our annual summer visit with family and friends.

Mike and I still bike together when he visits us from his home in Seattle. Biking has become an important part of his rehab as well.

For me, biking has been a vehicle for seeing the world up close and personal, either alone or in a group. Much of who I am is a result of my biking experiences. It provides a different perspective on life than traveling the interstate in an automobile.

Bike Schedule

I have been a dedicated biker for almost seventy years and plan to continue for as long as my body and mind hold out. Jan has threatened to have a GPS chip inserted in me so she can find me if I get lost while biking. So far I've always found my own way home.

My schedule for the past few years has been to go on long rides (thirty to forty miles) three or four days per week and golf on non-biking days. On my golf days, I often start or end the day with a shorter ride in the neighborhood. My cell phone is always on the handlebar and readily available for business as I bike. I carry a notepad and pencil to jot down messages or thoughts I want to remember or write about. I often run real estate errands on my bike, such as turning on lights in a listed home prior to a scheduled showing. I've been known to meet buyers at one of our listed homes, arriving on my bike. I have become known by some as the biking/blogging realtor—or something like that.

Biking may tend to tame our egos. It is my belief that if world leaders and politicians spent more time biking and less time bullying, the world would be a better place, with less violence, wars, poverty, pollution, terrorism, and crime.

A Brief History of My Writing

I started writing while in high school, as co-editor of the school newspaper and yearbook. My dream was to work for an award-winning newspaper like the *Louisville Courier Journal*, which I delivered. I read that newspaper cover to cover every day, and I had plans to major in journalism at the Ernie Pyle School of Journalism at IU, until older siblings persuaded me that journalism was an uncertain way to make a living. I took their advice and opted for economics and then law school. There were times in my career when I was unhappy with my work and wished I had followed my journalism dream. I've often wondered if I made the best decision, but today I have few regrets. In retrospect, I am content with the career paths I have taken.

Over the years, I have retained my love for writing. The favorite part of my law practice involved writing legal opinions and research briefs, creating legal documents, or writing letters to or on the behalf of clients.

As a young attorney representing a bank trust department, I wrote a monthly publication that was designed to promote estate and financial planning. *Agenda* was subsequently purchased by about a dozen other bank trust departments around the United States and adapted to their own trust staffs. It was my first attempt at creative writing.

During the last ten years of my law practice, I had the opportunity to serve on the board of three not-for-profit organizations. Attorneys are not universally loved, but charitable organizations love to have attorneys on their boards. On a couple of occasions, I had the opportunity to draft booklets that were used by these organizations in the service of their clientele.

Writing a monthly newsletter has been part of my responsibility for the past twelve years of our real estate business. It has been an effective marketing tool for the Boeglin Team and has kept our friends, neighbors, and other realtors informed about the housing market in our area.

I take opportunities to write poems and spoofs for family events, such as reunions or birthday celebrations. One of my favorites was a spoof I wrote for my brother Bob's eightieth birthday gathering. It was entitled "Bob Boeglin ... the Early Years." It has become a keepsake within the family.

My family has come to expect that Uncle Jim will be providing some of the entertainment for such events by creating a special publication.

Journaling has been an important part of my daily life for almost forty years, and I started blogging eight years ago. I have been told that I am a better writer than a speaker. I choose to accept that as a compliment on my writing rather than a slam on my speaking ability. Clearly, I get something out of putting my thoughts down on paper.

This story is an attempt to structure some of the musings I have entertained and lessons I have learned over seventy-four years of living, sixty-nine years of biking, almost sixty years of writing, thirty-five years as an attorney, and thirteen years in real estate. I am exploring such topics as insights learned from biking, what I learned while growing up in a small town, being an active participant in the aging process, religious and/or spiritual experiences, and observations on the American legal and political systems.

It seems to me that anyone who successfully navigates life's journey employs at least one vehicle to transport him or herself along the way. For me the bicycle and writing have both been helpful in keeping me moving in a positive direction. For others, it might be performing, playing a musical instrument, participating in a sport or hobby, engaging in a scientific pursuit, teaching, farming, hunting, fishing, a medical or professional career, cooking, care-taking, or any number of vehicles at our disposal. Whichever vehicle we select helps us to move forward and (hopefully) upward on our journey.

I am writing this story in large part to help me better understand and appreciate my own life journey. You are welcome to join me for the ride and maybe pick up some new insights for your own trip through life.

Jim Boeglin
Bonita Springs, Florida

CHAPTER 1

Ferdinand Roots

It Took a Village

What if our forefathers had lacked
the courage to leave what was known,
crossing a dangerous ocean
to American wilderness largely unknown?

Would we be here or even exist?
How could they have traveled so far?
Might we have been
caught in the web
of that Old World of conflict and war?

jb

Land of Lincoln

Ferdinand is in the southwest quadrant of Indiana, between Louisville and Evansville and about twenty miles north of the Ohio River. The terrain is hilly and wooded.

Before Ferdinand existed, Abraham Lincoln and his family lived less than ten miles away. The family had moved from Kentucky to Indiana, eventually continuing on to Illinois. Abe lived in a log cabin on Little Pigeon Creek, a tributary of the Ohio River, from 1816 to 1830—his formative years. It was on an excursion down the Ohio and Mississippi to New Orleans that Abe was first exposed to slavery. The slave market where human beings were being sold made a lasting impression on this future president.

The Lincoln Boyhood National Memorial is located just west of Ferdinand and marks the grave of Abe's mother, Nancy Hanks Lincoln. I spent many summer days during the '50s at the Lincoln State Park Beach. Ferdinand did not have a community swimming pool, and Lincoln State Park was the nearest available place for Ferdinand kids to safely swim. It was an easy bike ride on lightly traveled roads.

European Roots

Ferdinand was settled in 1840, which was ten years after Abe left for Illinois. It was settled by Europeans traveling down the Ohio River in search of a New World that reminded them of their Old World. The rolling, wooded hills of Southern Indiana closely resemble the Bavarian region of Germany.

In the one hundred and seventy-five plus years since its founding, there has not been a lot of diversification in Ferdinand. The townspeople remain virtually 100 percent Catholic and of German or Swiss ancestry. When I was a child in the '40s and '50s, many of the older generation were bi-lingual, switching back and forth between English and German seemingly at random. One of my first grade classmates spoke only German and had to learn English in elementary school. We initially thought Albert was not very smart, but he later proved us wrong as he became fluent in English. I never became fluent in German but seem to have an ear for understanding the spoken language.

Dad's ancestors were from the Alsace Lorraine Region of Europe that is now part of Switzerland. Mom's ancestors came from the Hamburg area of Northern Germany.

The official 1950 population of Ferdinand was 990, not counting the farmers who surrounded the town. At age seven, I knew everyone in town, and most of the farmers. Everyone seemed to know me. Interstate 64 wasn't even in the planning stages when I left for college in 1961. The town was truly "in the middle of nowhere."

Ferdinand was a pretty good place for a child to grow up. It was clean, safe, quiet, and comfortable. As children we were free to roam on our own at a very early age. No one worried about traffic, drugs, child molesters, or shootings. By age eight, I was encouraged to set out on my bike (after mass) on summer mornings. Sometimes I would not return home until it was time for 5:00 p.m. supper. Everyone in town looked out for everyone else.

Diversity and critical thinking were not among Ferdinand's strengths back then. It was a white world without any African Americans, Native Americans, Latinos, Asians, Jews, Protestants, Hindus, Muslims, or any form of minority. According to my brother Bob the only college graduates were Dr. Backer, Dr. Gutgsell, Dr. Metzger, Dr. Brackman, Albert Sonderman, Ed Madlon, and Elizabeth Hollinden. They made up less than .1 percent of the population.

Ferdinand of the '50s would prove to be a stifling environment for someone who wanted a wider experience of life. Questioning authority was strongly discouraged. It seemed to me that many of the people just wanted to be told how to think and what to believe. I had a different vision for my life.

For me, Ferdinand was a great place to be from. I had my eye on larger horizons from about age ten. I loved my family and friends, but I cannot remember a time in my childhood when I seriously considered spending my adult life in Ferdinand. My parents made it clear that there was a larger world out there and that life did not end at the city limits. I had permission to pursue my goals, wherever that might take me.

Unlike many small rural towns, Ferdinand has grown and prospered since I moved away. Now, many decades later, it is a growing and vibrant town and a great place to visit. My nephew Tim often referred to it as "God's country."

No Place to Hide

My parents took Catholicism seriously, and required that I attend daily mass even during the summers when school was out. I also took my turns as an altar boy. They had hopes that I would become a priest, a plan I did not share.

Attending mass became, for me, a time to daydream about being a major-league pitcher or basketball star. I was able to go through the motions of the mass without really being there.

I remember a few summer mornings when I was sick and tired of spending my time at the morning mass. I chose to spend the time biking around town until mass was over and then returned home, pretending to have been in church. It rarely worked out for me. Someone would usually rat me out. I soon learned to ride my bike outside of town, where fewer people would see me or know me.

Other times I would hide out in a back pew, hoping to avoid having to sing in the choir with the girls—I was painfully shy around girls until my last two years in high school. Inevitably, a nun would spot me and escort me up to the front of church to join the choir. They were on the lookout for "rebels." It was becoming more and more clear that I was not priestly material.

The Star Theater

An old fire trap served as the only movie theater in Ferdinand. It had less than one hundred seats, most of them with bubblegum stuck underneath them. The Star did not get first-run movies.

The ticket price for a kid was fourteen cents. My parents would give me fifteen cents, and I would use the extra penny for hard candy. Popcorn was out of my price range. By the time I was ten years old, ticket prices had climbed to fifteen cents, and that was the end of my hard candy. It was my first introduction to the economic concept of inflation.

The pattern was for a news reel, followed by cartoon and a scary serial like *The Iron Claw*, and finally the movie. Ma and Pa Kettle were favorites, as were many "Oaters" with Roy Rogers, Dale Evans, Gene Autry, and Hopalong Cassidy.

The owner/projectionist, "Snap" Quante, doubled as the bouncer. When behavior got out of hand, he would turn off the projector, walk up the aisle, and escort troublemakers out of the theater. In Ferdinand, bad behavior was limited to general rowdiness, throwing popcorn, and talking too loud. I seldom got into trouble because I knew that my parents would find out.

The Star Theater was the cultural center of the entire town, until it closed when I was about twelve years old. Fortunately, televisions began popping up in homes around town about that time. There was probably a connection between the advent of television and the demise of the theater.

What's in a Name?

Small towns seem to inspire nicknames. I remember Ferdinand guys with such nicknames as Bouncer, Durtch, Cheesy, Bobo, Goach, Snipe, Dippy, Snap, Booby, Petsy, Lefty, Cotton, Sonny, Spike, Popeye, Punky, Bonetickler, Bubbles (he wore thick glasses), even Turd (it started out Turtle because he moved so slowly but got shortened). I have often wondered what impact the nicknames had on the self-esteem of the individuals.

I never earned a nickname. However, I had been known by my middle name my entire life up until the seventh grade. I was Jim. During religion class one day, Father David let my entire seventh grade class know that my first name was actually George. As only kids can do, they decided to call me George from that day forward. My family and close friends stuck with Jim. It felt like an identity crisis to me, and when I went to Indiana University, I immediately reverted to Jim. I find nothing wrong with the name George, but it just isn't me. I've never totally forgiven Father David for what he did, and now it's too late for me to hear his confession.

Small-Town Characters

Small towns also seem to spawn memorable characters. My brother Jack loved to tell stories about some of the local characters. Jack lived his entire life (except his stint in Korea while in military service) in Ferdinand and would not have moved away if someone had offered him $1,000,000. He and Delores raised their four children, Brett, Todd, Stacey, and Curt, in a house next to the *Ferdinand News,* a weekly newspaper. Jack drove an RC Cola truck, and Delores worked as office manager at the *Ferdinand News*. Her commute to work was about twenty steps.

I wish Jack was still here to tell his stories. I miss him, and he would have a lot to add to this section. Unfortunately, he is one of the Boeglin boys who has completed his human journey.

The *Ferdinand News* was owned by two brothers, Oscar and Roy Haake. Oscar was the business manager, and Roy was the reporter. Roy wrote a playful weekly gossip column entitled "The Bull Spreader" in honor of Ferdinand the Bull. He wrote in an almost illiterate style that would have driven a spell-checker crazy. It was part Appalachian, part redneck, part hillbilly, and a little German thrown in for good measure.

Everyone was fair game, as Roy innocently reported the happenings around town. There was nothing mean-spirited about his reporting, and I doubt that any of his subjects were ever upset with his comments. It was considered an honor to be mentioned in

"The Bull Spreader." His column was probably part of the reason I wanted to become a journalist. Roy inspired me to want to write, and I was in awe of his creative writing ability.

Snipe was legendary. He came from a poor family, and his mother had died when Snipe was a small child. Snipe was raised by an unpopular stepmother, and his hair lip and cleft palate were never medically treated. He was very popular with his buddies, even though they sometimes made fun of the way he talked. Snipe was one of the very few young men in town who owned a car. He had dropped out of high school to work. His car was considered an important transportation source by his buddies, and they treated him well. Everyone would pile into the car and head to Jasper to the Family Drive-in Movie Theater (appropriately named because many families got their start at the drive-in). Snipe's trunk was useful for smuggling in passengers who did not have money for a ticket. Snipe eventually moved to Evansville but returned often to entertain his friends.

Bernie was a decorated war hero during the Allied invasion of Italy during WWII. Although I never read the book, I was told that he was featured in a well-known novel about the invasion. I remember him as rough and tough—a guy who could instill fear without even trying. After the war, he returned to Ferdinand and started a family and a sheet metal business. His family lived in an apartment behind the business.

Bernie was on my paper route, and it was always a challenge to collect for the paper. With a rapidly growing family, he rarely had enough money to catch up on what he owed me, and I was intimidated by him. He was killed in an industrial accident, still ten dollars in arrears on my bill. My recollection is that Bernie died after falling off the roof of a factory. He survived the invasion of Italy, only to fall to his death in peacetime.

Leon was an early basketball star at St. Ferdinand High School. In the 1950s, school consolidation had not yet taken hold in rural Indiana. Many towns, even smaller than Ferdinand, had high schools with less than one hundred students in the entire school. They were our competitors in basketball. Some of the rural gyms near Ferdinand were extremely small with relatively low ceilings.

Neighboring Bristow High School used a converted barn for their gymnasium. It had a pot-bellied stove for heat. The scorekeeper sat above the basketball floor and manually put up the score anytime there was a basket. Leon liked to shoot long, arching set shots from midcourt. I remember seeing him knock the popcorn out of the hands of the score keeper, spilling the popcorn all over the court, and causing a delay of game. Worst of all, the shot did not go in.

Indiana did not have a class system in sports based upon the size of schools. A school of any size had the same opportunity to win a state championship. Milan High School, with a town population of 1,150 and an enrollment of 161 students, won the Indiana State Basketball Championship in 1954, beating Indianapolis Crispus Attucks with Oscar Robertson, Terre Haute Gerstmeyer, and Muncie Central along the way. Milan was the inspiration for the 1986 film *Hoosiers*. It was also the inspiration for many small town basketball players, including me. I watched the state finals that year at the home of a neighbor, who had one of the first televisions in town. I was 11 years old and aspiring to become a star.

Another Ferdinand basketball star, Josie, was a very aggressive player. Unlike Leon, who shot from midcourt, Josie would barrel through the defense and shoot layups. Unfortunately, there was never a lot of room to stop behind the basket. Most of the gyms had a wall just a few feet beyond, and Josie crashed into many a wall during his high school career. I often wondered if banging his head against walls would affect his mental capacity later in life.

My cousin Wayne was an engineer and an entrepreneur. He didn't really fit into Ferdinand society and lived in a large home several miles from town. His engineering firm was headquartered on Main Street across from Fleigs Tavern. Wayne was rumored to own a chain of restaurants and nursing homes and flew his own airplane. He liked to hang around the taverns and drink beer with the locals.

Wayne was a stickler for Ferdinand traditions, which included a strict no-tipping policy in the taverns. When strangers wandered into town and violated such a policy, Wayne would be there to straighten them out. I remember one time when he grabbed the tip off the bar and threw the money into the window of the car of the astonished visitors, saying, "We're not going to start that s### around here!"

Lack of Organized Activities

Aside from Little League and scouting, kids in Ferdinand were pretty much on their own for activities. There were no soccer moms or swim teams or any other form of activity to keep kids out of trouble. We were on our own.

My friends and I would go from house to house on our bikes, encouraging kids to participate in a basketball game in our backyard, a touch football game on Stallings lot, or a baseball game at the city ball diamond. If we could entice a large enough group, we chose sides and played. Otherwise, we shot baskets on our own or took turns pitching a baseball to one another. We learned to be self-reliant and independent.

Our Very Own High School

Ferdinand girls were allowed to attend high school at the academy, a private school operated by the Benedictine nuns at the Convent of the Immaculate Conception. The academy was less than a mile from our home, and local girls could live at home while attending high school.

The academy attracted Catholic girls from Central and South America. Ferdinand was considered a safe environment to send troubled teenage girls away to school. I mean, what kind of trouble could a teenage girl find in a place like Ferdinand?

Both of my sisters, Mary Jo and Ann, were graduates of the academy. Mary Jo could type ninety words per minute on an old manual typewriter and became a secretary. Ann went on to become a registered nurse.

Until the '50s, the nearest high school for boys was in Huntingburg, and Ferdinand boys rode the Ferdy Flyer train or Harry Kippenbrock's school bus to school. Not everyone bothered with high school, and very few opted for a college education.

The Ferdy Flyer was an old steam engine (later replaced by a diesel locomotive) that hauled timber, students, and other products between Ferdinand and Huntingburg—less than ten miles.

During WWII my brother Bob became the bookkeeper for the train company while he was still a student at Huntingburg High School. The regular bookkeeper had been drafted, and Bob was a sophomore in high school. It was the beginning of his legendary career in accounting and banking. When the regular bookkeeper came back from the war, Bob was out of a job—probably the one and only time he was ever fired.

When I was in grade school, St. Ferdinand Parish raised the money to build a Catholic high school in town. My dad was instrumental in this movement, although he was in favor of a public high school. He lost that argument to the bishop in Evansville.

The school was largely funded from proceeds of an annual church picnic that raised money from raffles of cars, homemade quilts, and other crafts. The church picnic was famous from Louisville to Evansville, and people brought their gallon jars to buy the turtle soup that was made in large kettles in the parking lot. The turtle soup contained real turtle meat that a parishioner caught on a safari to Tennessee each summer. Beef and lots of fresh vegetables supplemented the turtle meat. The soup's recipe also included bourbon and red wine. It was great soup, and I remember it well.

The yellow brick high school building and gymnasium were a big source of town pride. The first year, about 1952, only freshmen and sophomores attended. Older kids continued to attend Huntingburg High School or the academy. My older brothers Bob, Tom, and Jack were all graduates of Huntingburg High School. My brother Joe, who became a CPA, was in one of the early classes to graduate in 1957. I was a member of the class of 1961. There were fifty-nine students in my graduating class.

Most of the teachers were priests or nuns, with a sprinkling of lay teachers who taught math and science and coached sports. Daily mass was held in the gymnasium and was mandatory. We knelt on the bleacher seats with nothing to lean on, which was sheer penance. Religion was an integral part of the curriculum. The sports teams were named the Crusaders, in honor of the Catholics who looted and pillaged the Middle East in the name of converting the infidels to Christianity.

The rumor was that St. Ferdinand High School was a great school academically. We really did not have anything to compare it to, so I can neither confirm nor deny the rumor. All I know is that very few graduates went on to college during my tenure.

For some reason our parents believed in the value of education, even though my mother, Clara, had only an eighth-grade education and my father, Otto, had just two years of high school at St. Meinrad Seminary before his dad died and he had to take over the family farm. They encouraged their children to pursue higher education, and their encouragement was rewarded. This humble base has produced medical doctors, dentists, attorneys, CPAs, CFOs, MBAs, nurses, engineers, therapists, directors of technology, computer technicians, stock brokers, social workers, school teachers, realtors, insurance agents, entrepreneurs, managers, and even a lieutenant governor of Indiana who is now a college president. But alas, no priests or nuns.

The Otto and Clara Boeglin Memorial Pergola

Over the past several years, individuals in Ferdinand, including my niece Sue and her husband Jim, were successful in saving an old Swiss-chalet home from the wrecking ball. A small group of people bought the Wollemann House and donated it to the Ferdinand Historical Society. Grants, donations, and volunteer labor restored the home to its former glory and it now houses a popular bistro.

Because of the prominence of my parents in the history of Ferdinand, our family was asked to fund the construction of the Otto and Clara Boeglin Memorial Pergola. Several of our nieces and nephews spearheaded the fund drive. The pergola now sits in the yard behind the Wollemann House and provides a venue for weddings, concerts, picnics, family reunions, and the like. It was dedicated at a Boeglin family reunion in 2015, with over one hundred descendants in attendance. The pergola is an indication of the love and respect that the descendants have for this remarkable couple even after all these years. Otto died in 1959, and Clara died in 1992.

CHAPTER 2

Lessons Learned from Catholicism

an all-encompassing religion

*What if God has no favorites
among Christians, Muslims, and Jews?
What if our God simply wants us
to be free to think and to choose?*

*Would we still argue for our own dogma,
to prove who's right and who's wrong?
Or would we live in harmony,
enjoying the beautiful song?*
jb

Religious Symbols

The dominant features of the town were (and still are) the large St. Ferdinand Catholic Church situated in the center of town on the second highest hill, and the Benedictine Convent of the Immaculate Conception atop the highest hill. I suppose the concept of building churches on hills has something to do with being that much closer to God.

The St. Ferdinand church has been lovingly restored over the years and is a reminder of some of the older churches in Germany. It seats approximately five hundred parishioners in its pews, with large stained-glass windows and the stations-of-the-cross on the interior walls. I didn't fully appreciate the beauty of the church in my early years, when my thoughts were on baseball, basketball, etc. Now when I go back to visit, I am thoroughly impressed.

The convent casts a shadow over the entire town, both literally and figuratively. It is actually a collection of large brick buildings known locally as "the castle on the hill." It has its own large church that rivals any church I've visited in Europe.

Some of the Benedictine nuns taught in the elementary school, even though it was a public school that just happened to be located adjacent to the church. No one objected to the public school being operated as a private Catholic school, as the whole town was Catholic. Daily mass was mandatory, as was religious education.

Mass was in Latin, and as an altar boy, I had to learn all the prayers and responses in Latin. A few of them still rattle around in my brain. Choir songs were sung in Latin. Prayer books were in Latin, with an English translation on the opposite page. Some of the older parishioners had the Latin translated into German instead of English.

The Benedictine Order of priests and nuns has roots back to sixth-century Europe, and the Ferdinand Convent and nearby St. Meinrad Archabbey were established during the nineteenth century. Education is a primary focus of the Order.

The nuns wore black habits that completely covered their bodies and white wimples that covered their heads except for eyes, nose, and mouth. The costume was not unlike the burkas worn by some Muslim women today. Most of the nuns were kind, caring school teachers or nurses; a few of them were mean, angry women. Discipline was never a problem in school.

While I was away in college in the turbulent sixties, some of the younger nuns "kicked the habit" and left the convent for more conventional lives. I've often wondered how they adapted to society after living in a nunnery since leaving grade school.

The convent was a convenient place for childhood adventure. During the winter, we would sled down the steep hill and through the cedar grove, all the way down to the nuns' cemetery near the bottom of the hill. In the summer, we would climb the big hill on our bikes and then race for about half a mile down the hill, past the church cemetery, past the grade school, and right across Main Street. Fortunately, there was not a lot of car traffic in those years. Biking down that hill at breakneck speed was Ferdinand's version of a roller coaster.

Many Sunday evenings involved special religious services, followed by a procession of several hundred people walking through the streets of town, praying the rosary. A visitor could have been forgiven for thinking he or she was in Germany or Spain or France. Other evenings included the stations-of-the-cross on the convent grounds.

There was a special park-like setting known as the Grotto that housed the stations, with gravel paths from one station to another.

Daily life in Ferdinand revolved around the Catholic Church, and it was a rare day that I was not in church at least once. Much of my first eighteen years were spent on my knees, and it was a humbling experience. I reached my life quota of religious participation at a very young age. By the time Laura and Mike had gone through First Communion, we were drifting away from the Church.

Large Families

Catholics were not supposed to use birth control, although the rhythm method was acceptable. By Ferdinand standards, a family with four children was considered a small family whose parents had good rhythm. Our family of seven was about average. Some of my friends came from families of twelve or more. My six siblings had twenty-eight children combined. Donna and I may have been the first members of either one of our families to resort to "illegal" birth control.

I worked one college summer with Sonny, who was the father of seventeen children. His wife and children ran the farm, and Sonny maintained roads and bridges for the county. Older children raised the younger ones. Somehow it all worked out.

Dr. Backer delivered a lot of babies, including twelve of his own. All seven of the Boeglins were born in our home on Main Street. The hospital in nearby Huntingburg was operated by the nuns of the Convent of the Immaculate Conception, but ironically it was rarely used for childbirth.

Religious Dogma

I have vivid memories of walking home from school and thinking about the religious beliefs being taught by the priests and nuns. Many of the concepts simply made no sense to me, but I had no one available to discuss my questions with me. Neither my parents nor anyone else were open to discussing my questions about Catholic teachings. It was taboo to question such strange teachings as:

- How did we get so lucky as to be born into the "one true church" that would get us to heaven? What about the Protestants, Jews, Muslims, Hindus, and nonbelievers who were also good people? Why were they denied entrance to heaven just because of their misguided religious beliefs?
- Why was I guilty for something Adam and Eve did long before I was born?
- Why was I constantly told that I was a miserable sinner? What did I do?
- Why did ending a marriage with a divorce doom you to hell?
- Who decided that the priests and nuns were infallible?
- If I was a really good person but died just after engaging in sex outside of marriage, would I really be punished with eternal damnation? (Fortunately or unfortunately, I did not have any prospects for committing such a sin at the time.)
- Why were the Russian and Chinese Communist indoctrinations of the '50s called brainwashing but the Catholic indoctrination was religious education? And didn't the priests and nuns live in communes?

I learned to keep my questions to myself until I got to Indiana University and felt free to talk about my misgivings. It was an authoritarian atmosphere in Ferdinand that discouraged critical thinking or asking questions. Only troublemakers were questioning.

Some of my favorite memories of IU are late nights spent sitting around a dorm room discussing religion, politics, and world affairs. Students from different backgrounds shared their own beliefs and non-beliefs. College life was a world apart from Ferdinand. I had finally found a home that allowed me the freedom of expression I had been missing.

Chapter 3

Lessons Learned
from Baseball

The National Pastime

The pitcher is wild, the catcher intense,
the infielders spread 'round the bases.
The batter is crouched, eyeing the fence.
Runners on bags retie laces.
A fastball comes right down the middle.
The bat meets the ball with a smash.
The runners take off, circling the bases.
The home crowd erupts as the ball clears the fence,
and the batter runs home in a flash.

Jb

The Cardinals

We lived in the Ohio River Valley, and summertime in Ferdinand
was hot and humid. Air conditioning was an unknown concept.

Before anyone in town had a television, baseball was an important summer activity.

Our family was fortunate to have an FM radio that allowed us to listen to the St. Louis Cardinals' games. The entire neighborhood would gather on our front porch to listen to Harry Caray and Gabby Street as they described the play by play. My heroes were Hall of Fame outfielder Stan Musial, second baseman Red Schoendienst, who later became manager, pitcher "Vinegar Bend" Mizell, and Enos Slaughter. I had to be quiet about being a Slaughter fan, as it was rumored that he was divorced. I wondered if he was going to hell.

Kids would play hide and seek or kick the can while keeping in touch with the progress of the game. We would watch for the mail plane to fly over town about 9:00 p.m. on its route from Louisville to St. Louis. That was the signal that it was bedtime. Our parents would tell us the final results of the ballgame in the morning.

Most people worked six days a week, with Sunday as the day of rest for everyone but the priests, paperboys, farmers, and mothers. Local businesses were required to be closed on Sundays. Mornings were to be spent in church, followed by a fried chicken dinner at home.

We spent summer afternoons at the ballpark. Ferdinand had a semipro team in the I-K (Indiana-Kentucky) League, named the Cardinals after the St. Louis team. Nearby towns in the I-K League included Huntingburg, Jasper, Tell City, Rockport, Cannelton, Owensboro, and Booneville. All games were played on Sunday afternoon.

The Boeglin Lumber Company, owned by our family, was a sponsor of the Cardinals, and my brother Bob was the center fielder when he was not away in college. I looked forward to Bob coming home from college as he and I spent time together, playing pitch and catch in the front yard. Bob is fourteen years older than me, and he was my hero. Come to think of it, he still is. Bob still has the baseball uniform with Boeglin Lumber Company on the back of the shirt, and he wore it to a family reunion a few years ago.

My own baseball career involved being a hotshot Little League pitcher before suffering a compound fracture of my right wrist in a 1956 roller skating fall. That was the end of my curve ball, and I finished my career as a catcher in high school and for the Jasper American Legion team. So much for my dreams of becoming a major-league pitcher! (I still couldn't concentrate during mass.)

The BBB

In the spring of 1970, I was a young attorney managing a trust department for a bank in Kokomo, Indiana. My brother Joe was a CPA in Anderson, Indiana, about thirty miles away. Brother Bob was a banker in Indianapolis, less than fifty miles from either of us. We all led busy lives, which made it difficult for us to get together on a regular basis. Bob and Mary were raising five children, Cathy, Bobby, Danny, Connie, and David; Joe and Betty had two small children, Phil and Amy; and my first wife, Donna, and I had Laura (two) and Mike (one). Bob tackled our separation issue through our mutual interest in baseball. He sent Joe and me an anonymous postcard with a simple message: Sid's Bar, Noblesville, Indiana, 7:00 p.m. Saturday. Be there!

No one made contact with anyone else, but Joe and I both showed up at the appointed time. We found Bob sitting at a table in the family dining room, with sheets of paper spread on the table. Before fantasy sports were invented, Bob had devised a fantasy baseball draft for the 1970 season. It eventually became known as the Boeglin Baseball Bonanza.

Bob is a talented mathematician, and statistics come naturally for him. He compiled a list of the best hitters in both the National and American Leagues in 1969, giving one point for every run batted in (RBI) and three points for every home run (HR). For the pitchers, he gave five points for every win they were credited in 1969. From that list, we took turns drafting 5 batters and 5 pitchers in each league as our fantasy players for the 1970 season. Bob then kept track of each player's points and provided worksheets monthly and at the end of the season. The winner got ten dollars from the other two players, and the loser had to buy the beer at the next draft.

That was the beginning of an annual family reunion that included all seven siblings or their spouses or children. Fantasy baseball was the excuse for getting the family together. Usually the clan gathered in Ferdinand, but a few memorable baseball drafts occurred in Indianapolis, Anderson, and Bonita Springs, Florida.

The Boeglin Baseball Bonanza occurred every year for over forty years, until there were only a few of us original siblings still running the bases.

CHAPTER 4

The German Work Ethic

Craftsmanship Matters

What if a job is not about filling time,
but doing a task well done?
What if the reward
for working hard
is a feeling that's almost like fun?

Jb

WWII

My earliest memories of Ferdinand are of young men having just returned home from serving in Europe or the Pacific during WWII. It must have been doubly difficult for these young men of German ancestry to fight the German war machine, and some of them were hailed as heroes.

The husband of my oldest sister, Mary Jo, was a tail gunner, I'm told on a B-29 bomber that flew missions over Japan. "Lip," a Ferdinand boy, was an interesting, likeable character who loved jazz music. They married shortly after the war was over, with the wedding reception in our unfinished basement and backyard. They went on to raise six sons, Steve, Bill, George, John, Jeff, and Fred.

Some of the town's young men did not return home from the war, and the cemetery is lined with their grave markers.

Work Ethic

Ferdinand may have been small, but it was (and still is) prosperous. Furniture factories benefitted from a labor force of skilled craftsmen who were steeped in the traditional German work ethic. Shirkers were not popular. Everyone worked hard and took great pride in what they did.

Homes were well maintained and lawns mowed, and the entire town was neat and clean. An outsider might have thought he or she had landed in Europe prior to the war.

Today the town is home to several large homegrown employers. The workforce far exceeds the population of the town, with workers descending on Ferdinand from neighboring towns. Residents of Ferdinand remain mostly the descendants of the German and Swiss immigrants who settled there in the nineteenth century.

I learned the work ethic very well, having had chores such as lawn mowing, berry picking, gardening, baling hay, delivering newspapers, and at age sixteen (two months after the death of my dad), I became warehouse boy for the 7Up distributor. It was a part of "becoming a man" and required that I give up basketball, which was not an easy decision.

After school, weekends, and summers were spent unloading the trucks of cases of empty bottles and loading them back up for the following day's routes. College summers were spent stacking lumber at the sawmill that had previously been known as the Boeglin Lumber Company, or working for the county highway department or in furniture factories in Jasper.

While at Indiana University, I had jobs in dormitory cafeterias, science labs, and the campus mailroom. I worked at an Indianapolis bank full time to earn my way through my final two years of night law school. My experience in the tax division of the trust department was invaluable when I was able to move into the practice of law.

I have not been without a job since age ten, and I thank my Ferdinand upbringing for teaching me to work hard and take pride in my job.

Authority Figures

Part of the German work ethic is simply to do as you're told. Authority figures play a big role in breeding productive citizens. There were no unions protecting the rights of the workers. In the furniture factories, everyone contributed as a member of a team. No one questioned the foremen or plant managers. They worked hard, did what they were told, and were thankful for the opportunity to be productive.

The Catholic clergy was clearly at the top of the power pyramid in Ferdinand. Father David was pastor, and he was pretty much "the king." He usually had two or three assistant priests who rotated through our church from the nearby St. Meinrad Archabbey. They lived in the rectory next to church and supervised the behavior of the parishioners.

Guilt was a strong motivator, and people were expected to confess their sins to a priest at least every other week. Slacking off at work would have been considered a sin. To my knowledge, no one questioned the priests' authority. Their word was the law. I always dreaded going into that little black box to confess my sins. Most of my sins involved impure thoughts, as impure actions were hard to come by in Ferdinand.

I learned to keep my questions to myself, sometimes posing the questions out loud only while biking by myself outside of town. The nuns who taught in school were also not to be questioned. We learned to keep quiet at home if we were disciplined in school. If our parents learned that we had earned the wrath of a nun, we were punished again at home. There were no justifications accepted. The nuns were right—period. Children also lacked a union to protect their rights.

The entire town watched out for the behavior of children. Everyone knew everyone else in town, and it was totally acceptable for an unrelated adult to discipline a child who was causing trouble. Corporal punishment was a way of life.

Children were to be seen and not heard. Adults were to be respected and obeyed, no matter what. Children had no rights.

It is hard to know for sure, but I am not aware of any predatory priests assigned to the St. Ferdinand parish. If there were any such scandals, they were kept secret from the children.

Taverns

In the Germanic tradition, this small town of less than a thousand people had five bars, and they were all booming. Fleigs was in an old building, and the owner, Ed Fleig, and his family lived upstairs above the bar. It was popular with pinochle players and did not have a family room in addition to the bar room. It was adults only. Fleigs was on my paper route. The old building has since been replaced with a bank branch.

The Oasis had a large family room and was run by Johnny Weyer, a well-liked bartender who had two sisters who were nuns. It was a very popular hangout for high school kids.

Carly's was a dive down the street from Church. It probably should have been closed down by the Health Department. The older men tended to patronize Carly's for card playing.

The Covered Bridge may have been the oldest building in town and was once an inn for travelers when Ferdinand was young. Sheepshead tournaments were a staple of the Covered Bridge.

The American Legion was located on the south end of Main Street and ironically had a large plastic bull on its roof in honor of Ferdinand the Bull, the fictional character in the children's book by Munro Leaf. Ferdinand the Bull was a pacifist who would rather smell flowers than fight.

Patrons would walk from one bar to another, greeting friends and guzzling beer. This was the focus of social activity in Ferdinand. Much of the wages earned through hard work in the factories ended up in these cash registers. Alcoholism was an unstated problem and perhaps a byproduct of the inability to question authority. Drinkers tended to drown their reservations in beer rather than discussing them openly.

The laws of the state of Indiana were not enforced in Ferdinand when I was a teenager. A sixteen-year-old boy with money in his pocket could sit at the bar and drink beer in any one of the five locations. As long as he did not cause trouble, he was welcome at the bar. Parents were usually aware of this activity and tolerated it. My mother was not aware of my participation, but she probably had her suspicions. Dad would have recognized the behavior, but he had died shortly after my sixteenth birthday.

My brother Jack worried about me when I graduated from law school. He knew I needed to become licensed to practice law, and he claimed he had never seen me "pass a bar." In truth, I rarely frequented bars once I was of legal age. I was too busy with work and school.

Before his death, one of my dad's assignments was to deliver beer to the priests on Saturday afternoons. It was not considered appropriate for the priests to be seen in the taverns with the common people. Between that beer and church wine, the priests managed to keep up with the townspeople. Father David was known to have a second chalice of wine at the 6:00 a.m. mass to calm his shaking hands.

Getting Out of Dodge

It was a red-letter day for me when I headed north to Bloomington at age eighteen, eager to begin my college experience at Indiana University. It was only seventy miles, but I was transitioning into a different world. I would have gladly biked the seventy miles pulling a wagon with my possessions, but my brother Joe drove me to school and introduced me to his friends in the dormitory. Joe was four years older than me and graduated just before I began my freshman year.

Like Joe, I was a resident scholar assigned to live in Upper Linden, an old army barracks that was converted to a dormitory after WWII. We did our own janitorial work, were required to have a job for a minimum of ten hours per week, and maintained at least a B average to remain eligible as a resident scholar. For this, our room and board was capped at $490 per semester. Upper Linden was the home of many of the top scholars at IU. My first roommate, Paul, made Phi Beta Kappa his junior year.

I did not return to Ferdinand until Christmas break and could hardly wait to get back to school. Except for my continuing contacts with Donna, I began to lose touch with my high school friends. Only one of my classmates, Skip, went to college right after high school, although two of the girls became nuns. Many of the boys went into the military, and some of them later attended college on the GI Bill.

For the first three summers of college, I returned to Ferdinand and lived with my mother while working to earn money for the next year of school. The summers could not pass quickly enough to suit me. My hay fever allergies made it miserable to be stacking lumber, and I missed my new friends from college. I felt like I was in a twilight zone. After I received my degree and entered law school, I only returned to Ferdinand for an occasional visit.

My first wife, Donna, probably wanted to get out of town as badly as I did. Following our marriage, we lived in Indianapolis, and she worked as an RN at the Indiana University Medical Center. I worked at the bank and attended IU Law School at night

One common denominator throughout my growing-up years was the bicycle. It provided me with the freedom to explore and question my world. It was my vehicle for moving on from life in Ferdinand to life at Indiana University and beyond. I have my sister Ann to thank for my early introduction to the bike. Maybe it is time for me to forgive her for abandoning me in favor of nurse's training.

CHAPTER 5

Finding True North

Lessons Learned While Biking

What if no one had dared
to design a two-wheeled vehicle?
Would we still be riding horses
or tooling around on a tricycle?

The bicycle offers a way
to travel without using fuel.
A much better option than horses,
not to mention an ass or a mule.

jb

A Role Model

Dr. Stephen Covey was an internationally known and respected educator, author, leader, and organizational expert. I was an avid fan of Dr. Covey long before I was aware that he was a fellow biker. He recently died at age seventy-nine because of a bicycle accident in

Rock Canyon Park, Provo, Utah. To me, seventy-nine is beginning to sound young. However, death due to a biking accident at that age does not sound like the worst way to exit this journey.

Dr. Covey's books, *Seven Habits of Highly Effective People* and *Principle-Centered Leadership*, have been important resources for me along the way. He partnered with Franklin Planner to develop the *Franklin Covey Planner*, which I have been using for as long as I can remember. It is a system that works well for me in organizing and tracking my schedule, goals, and activities. It provides me with an organized system for living a focused life.

The concept of true north is a central principle of Steven Covey's life and his teachings. I have made it a guiding principle in my business and personal life. I have come to learn that natural laws and principles are not always obvious. The world most of us see is really a reflection of our internal frame of reference. In any given situation, we look inside and decide what we want to see. We then project that view out to determine the truth as we see it. What we see is not always true north.

Stephen Covey was well aware that different people viewing the identical situation might see the truth differently based on their internal frame of reference. This is never more obvious than during a political election. Our internal values can skew the concept of true north to meet our desires and emotional needs. The same political candidate can be loved and respected by some and loathed as a dangerous, vulgar joke by others.

The United States has just survived a presidential campaign that polarized our citizens at an unprecedented level. Both ends of the political spectrum strongly believe that their candidate was right and the other candidate was a crook. Families have been torn apart because of the campaign. Surely not everyone can be right in their evaluation of the candidates—or can they?

Another example is different people seeing a biker along the road can have an entirely different view of the biker. One motorist may react angrily and lay on his horn or squeeze the biker off the road. Another motorist may look at the biker and admire a fellow human being who is making an effort to be physically fit. Yet another person may see the biker and wish she could ride along. The underlying fact is that it is just a biker riding alongside the road, totally oblivious to the perspectives of the other people.

Conversely, two bikers riding together might see someone walking his or her dog along the path. The first biker may react with fear that the dog will attack him. The second biker may have the urge to stop and pet this beautiful animal. It is the same dog for both bikers, who happen to be seeing the dog through different filters.

Being aware of this process can be the insight that allows us to consciously choose how we want to react to any given situation. To me, that is the True North Principle—we are free to choose, and our choice has the potential to be helpful or hurtful—to ourselves and others. Fear and anger are usually not true north perspectives, but love and kindness usually point in that direction. A true north perspective encourages us to do the right thing.

Temperament

To me, temperament means our basic nature, character, natural tendencies, etc. There is no right or wrong temperament. We are all different. That is the essence of human nature.

On a scale from one (extreme introvert) to ten (raging extrovert), I consider myself to be a three or four. Occasionally I bike with a group, but the vast majority of my six thousand miles per year are logged alone. I view biking as a solitary sport that feeds my need for alone time. Golf is my social sport.

I have chosen careers that are dominated by extroverts—the legal profession and real estate sales. Writing and biking are my counterbalance from the everyday business of functioning as an extrovert. It is a quiet time for me to go inside and stay in touch with my personal true north.

Being on my bike awakens my inner child. As an experienced bicyclist, I have sufficient skill to maneuver on winding trails, race fellow bikers for a playful mile or two, or just go with the flow of the journey. The aches and pains I used to associate with jogging are relatively minor on the bike. My knees are free of pain, and I usually have a smile on my face as I ride. Apparently my temperament is well-suited for being a biker.

Biking offers unique opportunities to grow and learn. It presents us with choices and allows us to choose true north or a different direction. Similar to golf, biking offers a wide array of experiences ranging from physical to mental, emotional, and spiritual.

Physical Workout

Maintaining physical fitness is a good idea no matter our age or situation. Physical conditioning contributes to healthy mental, emotional, and spiritual states of consciousness. Jogging, walking, swimming, and biking are generally considered excellent vehicles for taking care of the health of our bodies.

Bicycling is one of the best ways for a person to stay physically fit with little chance of injury to the body. Barring an accident, such as a fall or collision, biking is gentle on the body. Knees and hips are spared the jarring impacts of jogging or even walking. Like swimming, it offers great cardio benefits, weight management, and muscle strength.

When I get passed by young bikers out for a "century,"—a one hundred mile ride, I marvel at the lean, narrow bodies and the muscular legs and arms. Somehow, no matter how long or how hard I bike, the biker's body eludes me. My heart, however, appears strong, and I feel physically fit and full of energy.

I have observed a growing number of men and women in our neighborhood who have taken up biking and over time have transformed their bodies from overweight to lean and mean. For me it is a pleasing miracle to watch in process. For them, it has been a way to improve the quality of their lives while extending their life span at the same time. I see more and more bikers in the neighborhood every year.

I was recently humbled by an encounter with another biker. We arrived at the same time for a rest on my usual bench at Venetian Village in Naples. We shared the bench and talked about our favorite bike routes in Bonita Springs and Naples. The man appeared to be at least eighty years old and had a biker's body that was lean, muscled, and trim. When it was time to get back on our bikes, I left first. About two minutes later, he passed me like I was going backwards. I watched his flashing rear light disappear in the distance, in awe of this magnificently conditioned athlete. I poured some cold water on my ego and kept biking.

Problem Solving

When I practiced law, the biggest part of my job was helping clients to solve problems. The problem might involve money, family relationships, business or employment issues, disputes, tax challenges, custody and support of children, purchase or sale of a business, estate planning, property division, contract negotiations, elder law decisions, abusive relationships, or all of the above. Some problems were easily resolved, with obvious legal answers. Sometimes, however, sticky emotional issues required creativity and thinking outside the box.

After my personal experience with divorce in 1987, I incorporated family mediation into my law practice. I became a certified family mediator during the last fifteen years of my law practice, helping couples to get through this difficult time as smoothly, easily, and inexpensively as possible.

For many years, courts in Fort Wayne required that divorcing couples or parents in custody disputes attempt mediation before a contested trial was allowed. This policy was partially to unclog crowded court schedules but also to encourage couples to cooperate and participate in resolving their own issues. The court was considered the last resort. Family mediators are usually attorneys or mental health professionals.

As an alternative to the adversarial process, family mediation is a kinder, gentler, less expensive way to dissolve a marriage. In my experience, the goal of family mediation is to help the spouses to identify issues in which they are already in agreement, so they don't spend energy, time, and money arguing over issues on which they already agree; then to identify, isolate, and define the issues in conflict.

The main focus of the mediation process is usually about finding mutually satisfactory solutions to the issues in conflict. It involves negotiation and compromise, rather than a fight followed by a heavy-handed decision by the court in which one party must win and the other must lose. The parties end up owning their settlement agreement, which makes it much less likely that the agreement will be breached after the divorce is final.

I remember one particularly angry couple who were represented by two of the nastiest divorce attorneys in Fort Wayne. No one was happy to be in mediation—including their attorneys, who were pushing them toward an expensive showdown in court. Mediation sessions involved lots of yelling and screaming, and had to be scheduled for evenings and weekends to avoid disrupting other tenants in my office building.

After a couple of required mediation sessions, we had (surprisingly) identified many areas of agreement on the financial issues. Only a few conflicting items remained unresolved involving the custody, support, and parental schedules with the minor children. As often happens, the kids were caught in the middle between two warring parents. However, I saw hope after finding so many areas on which they actually agreed.

A third and final mediation was scheduled for Saturday morning, and a sleepless night was not helpful in my quest to find a solution.

However, during an early morning bike ride, some potential answers began to surface in my mind. I went to the office and put my thoughts into the working draft mediation agreement, just in case the parties might agree. Nearly an hour into that final mediation session, a common light bulb went on, and they both reached the same conclusion that I had reached on my bike ride. I pulled out the mediation agreement, and they both signed. Their attorneys' battle plans were scuttled, and the adults had a blueprint for co-parenting their children. It was a win/win for everyone but their attorneys.

An Adversarial Divorce

Another problem-solving opportunity presented itself as a result of a contempt action filed by a father after the mother, my client, refused to allow court-ordered overnight visitation arrangements for their two small girls. This had been an adversarial divorce, and neither parent was happy with the other one.

It seems the father lived in an apartment and kept an arsenal of guns in an unlocked closet. When the girls told their mother about the guns, she decided it was too dangerous a condition for the girls, ages seven and five, to spend overnights with their father. She refused to allow the girls to spend the night unless he locked up the guns. He refused to lock up his guns in the girls' presence and filed for contempt of court against his ex-wife for violating the court order that allowed him overnight visitation. He also asked for sole custody because the mother was obviously "unfit to parent."

The father hired a notorious gunslinger attorney to press his case. A hearing was set, and I was wrestling with how to defend against the aggressive attacks the attorney would take on my client. The answer came to me on a bike ride. Be defenseless!

I prepared my client to be non-defensive against the attorney's attacks and let him ramble, no matter how painful it might be for her. Her only role was to be truthful and polite. I knew the judge was a father with small children of his own, and I trusted his judgment in this situation. The nastier the father's attorney became, the better it would be for my client.

We stipulated the facts of the case and let the examination commence. After thirty minutes of relentless, merciless attacks on the mother of these two little girls, she was in tears but did not fight back.

When the attorney finished with her, the judge asked me if I wanted to examine the witness. I declined and simply rested the defense. The judge then proceeded to lecture the father about his responsibilities as a parent, denied his request for custody and contempt, and ruled that he could visit with his daughters only if he locked up his guns while the children were in his presence.

Sometimes the best defense is defenselessness.

Spirituality and Religion

Jan and I have been traditional churchgoers for much of our lives. She grew up Presbyterian, and I grew up Catholic. Other times of our lives we have looked to alternative ways to experience our spiritual natures. We do not consider spirituality and religion to be necessarily the same thing. Religion can be a helpful avenue for a person to get in touch with their spirituality. It can also be a hindrance, if the religious approach is to dictate dogma and use the pulpit to gain power over others. I have experienced both approaches in my lifetime.

Jan and I initially met in 1981 when she was a sales representative for Safeguard Business Systems. I functioned as the managing partner of our law firm, and Jan sold me an accounting system for the firm. I saw her a few times in the ensuing years as she provided assistance to our bookkeeper, who was responsible for the accounting system. Then she disappeared from my life to become sales and marketing director of her family's marshmallow business.

In early 1987, I was looking for spiritual nourishment while going through a painful divorce with Donna. As a divorcing (and recovering) Catholic, I did not feel comfortable turning to my religion of origin.

One Sunday morning, to my own surprise, I simply showed up at the Unity Church in Fort Wayne. I made an immediate connection with the minister, Claudette, who was a former Catholic nun. She had a way of communicating without preaching. She made me think, and I liked her open, non-judgmental message. I returned to Unity the following Sunday, and there was Jan. She was an active member of the congregation, and single. The rest is history.

We were both involved members of the congregation for many years, including terms on the board of trustees. Since moving to Florida, we have found alternate ways to connect with our spiritual aspects. For me, an early morning ritual that includes watching the sun rise over the golf course behind our house, inspirational reading, journaling, and meditation helps to keep me spiritually focused and grounded.

My Catholic mother once asked me if we attended church regularly. I told her that we were currently attending the Church of the Bike, spending many Sunday mornings biking through parks and connecting with God through nature and each other. She liked the idea and expressed regret that she never learned to ride a bike.

Sometimes, while riding a quiet trail in a nature setting, the repetitive pedaling of the bike moves me into a mystical state of consciousness. It provides an inner peace that can otherwise be difficult to attain during a busy, hectic lifestyle. The ego chatter of the mind is released, at least for a while, and a higher consciousness prevails.

Emotional Balancing Act

Life has its ups and downs. I know very few people who feel up all the time. I do know a few people who seem to feel down all the time—sad victims of the world. I do my best to be non-judgmental of their process, while maintaining a safe distance just in case this condition is contagious. Most of us go with the flow of life and make an effort to enjoy life's experiences as much as possible. Some days are good; some days are challenging.

I cannot remember a bad day on the bike. It's like taking a happy pill. No matter the challenges going on in my life, a bike ride seems to put things into perspective. I find it almost impossible to feel down when I am moving forward on my bike, and the positive feelings linger long after the ride is over.

Biking is a relatively easy activity for most people to take up. Within weeks a new biker can be exploring the neighborhood and getting into shape at the same time.

Like everyone else I know, I have experienced difficult challenges in my lifetime—such issues as the deaths of parents, parents-in-law, two brothers, two sisters, three nephews, and close friends; an agonizing dissolution of a twenty-year marriage; leaving an established law partnership to venture out into my own legal practice; health issues that required open-heart bypass surgery; and the everyday challenges and disappointments that life throws at each of us. I have used biking as a vehicle to process these challenges and to move forward with my life.

Overcoming Limitations/Fears

Many psychologists agree that fear is the primary emotion behind other negative emotions. Perhaps the biggest obstacles to a happy, meaningful life are the irrational fears we carry with us as heavy emotional baggage on our journey.

Many of us (me included) have been programmed to fear from an early age. We fear God, hell, authority figures, death, other people, being rejected, failing, financial disaster, looking stupid, new or scary situations, and uncertainties. As a child, fear and guilt were strong emotions in my life. I felt guilt for being a sinner by Catholic standards; fear of going to hell; fear of being a failure; fear of disappointing my parents; and fear of the unknown.

Our fears often manifest as shyness, stress, worry, depression, insecurity, anger, arrogance, defensiveness, selfishness, bigotry, greed, discrimination, bullying, attack, and a general unwillingness to explore new adventures, limiting activities to our comfort level. Unless we learn to overcome our fears, we miss out on much of the good stuff life has to offer.

The simple act of riding a two-wheeled bicycle requires an element of mastering fear. Whether we are small children or adults when we are introduced to the bicycle, fear is a natural reaction to the thought of keeping such a vehicle upright and moving under our control. We must trust our ability to do so or forego the freedom and pleasure that a bike affords.

Overcoming fears tends to be a lifelong process. I believe our willingness and ability to move through our fears ultimately defines the quality of our lives.

Biking can be an important vehicle for mastering fears. It allows us to move outside our normal boundaries and trust that the world really is a friendly place that is populated by good people, many of whom may not look exactly like we look, have a slightly different skin color, or believe differently than we do. I regularly bike through neighborhoods that I would never see in any other way. It feels good to acknowledge and talk with people who would otherwise not be a part of my world.

Biking in Germany was a two-week master's level course on dealing with our fears. Our group of four (Dave, Sandy, Jan, and I) took our own bikes, which had to be disassembled in the United States and boxed for the flight. My first fear was that we would not be able to successfully reassemble the bikes at the Frankfort airport. Then we had to get them loaded with our luggage and onto trains for the trip to Heidelberg, all the while figuring out train schedules in a foreign language. Once in Heidelberg, we had to trust that we could find accommodations as we began our bike trek along the Romantic Road with minimal ability to speak or understand German and no reservations anywhere.

Every step along the way presented stressors, making biking fifty to sixty miles per day the easy part of the trip. Through trial and error, we learned to function as a team. (It helped that Dave is a psychologist.) The people we met were extremely friendly and eager to help four Americans who appeared to be lost much of the time. They provided lessons in map-reading, places to stay the night, time schedules for ferry crossings of rivers, which castles were worth touring, and favorite pubs.

Somehow, we always found comfortable, inexpensive "zimmers" (like American B & Bs) to spend the night. Full-bodied German beer was always available to numb the pain from being on the bike much of the day.

We followed the Romantic Road, which traces the old Roman trail through Germany before it was a country. The fortressed city of Rothenberg is on the Romantic Road and was probably the highlight of the trip for me. We spent an extra day exploring this ancient city and found a conveniently comfortable zimmer above a tavern to spend a couple of nights.

Ultimately, we had to find our way back to the Frankfort airport for our return flight, bikes suitably disassembled and boxed for transport. We managed to deal with every fearful unknown and experienced the trip of a lifetime. Those memories are now etched in our minds, and we are different people for having pushed our boundaries to new limits.

Helping Others

It is a well-recognized principle that giving is more powerful than receiving. From the Bible to various spiritual belief systems, helping others is a basic tenet. In my experience, people who are consistent givers—of their time, talents, and treasure—are the happiest people I know. People who focus on getting are often quite miserable, no matter how much they receive or take. They can never get enough to feel satisfied, much less happy.

Bikers may tend to be loners, but they really are a kind, friendly, generous lot. We acknowledge each other on the trail. As we bike, it is not unusual to come upon a biker in distress, either due to an accident or a breakdown, such as a flat tire. Most fellow bikers stop to see if help is needed. Sometimes all that is needed is kindness and support. Other times, it may be sharing a Band-Aid or a tool, or holding a wheel while a new inner tube is inserted. The simple act of being there for another person inevitably lifts the spirit of the person in need and also the person helping out.

As I biked north on Three Oaks Parkway, I noticed a biker ahead of me who was signaling for me to stop. He told me there was broken glass ahead, and he was concerned that a biker would suffer a flat tire. Together, we cleaned up the broken glass and disposed of it in a safe place. We were looking out for our fellow bikers and the feeling we got working together was priceless.

Recently I came upon a young couple sitting alongside the road, trying to deal with a flat tire. I stopped and asked if I might help. They gladly accepted my offer, as they clearly had no idea how to fix the flat. The young man had been trying to get the new inner tube inside the tire without success. I was able to hold the tire while showing him the proper technique, and we were all back on our bikes ten minutes later. I enjoyed my short time with these young folks, and it felt wonderful to be helpful. For me, it was the highlight of that day's ride.

Many bikers participate in events to raise funds for a charitable cause. Often they pay an entry fee for the privilege of volunteering to be a fund raiser. I have yet to meet a biker who resented having to pay for the privilege of giving. The giver is inevitably the receiver of the gift.

Freedom

Some sports activities require learning lots of rules and remembering disciplines—things like "keep your eye on the ball" or "keep the elbow in" or "keep your head still." Similar to jogging and walking, biking has only a few "rules of the road." Once we master keeping the bicycle upright and moving in a desired direction, we're good to go.

Early in my life, the bicycle was my ticket to freedom. It was the resource that allowed me to explore my hometown and the surrounding areas. It loosened the tether to home and expanded my independence.

Today the easy roll of the bike provides me with a profound sense of moving freely. Biking is one of the few ways a person in his or her seventies can move quickly and without effort. I am free to decide where I will bike, for how long, at what speed, and with or without companionship. With no rules to weigh me down, my mind is free to float in any direction. I can run errands along the way or stop for breakfast or lunch. When I get tired, I can stop and rest.

Like many of my fellow bikers, I have a carrying bag on the handle bars and bungee cords on the rear rack. If I need more cargo space for grocery store or hardware store items, I can put panniers on the back rack and triple my carrying capacity. I get a feeling of satisfaction from running errands on my bike rather than getting in the car.

Adventure

A sense of adventure is sadly lacking in many people's lives. As we age we tend to get stuck in the ruts of daily living. Youthful dreams may fade as our lives narrow down to fewer options. From riding a bicycle, I have learned that the unexpected lurks around every corner. The adventure is limited only by my own energy and imagination. I go places on my bike that I would never see in any other way.

Biking in Europe was a life-changing adventure. We met new people, learned to communicate despite language barriers, and explored a world much different than Indiana. There was an altogether different "feel" of a culture that was more than a thousand years old, with families living in the same homes and small towns for generations. Visiting castles and walled cities, it was easy to get a sense of the long history of the people.

When Mike and I biked from Bonita Springs through much of the state of Florida, we never knew what kind of biking conditions would prevail on the next leg. We didn't know exactly where we would be spending the night but trusted that we would be safe.

We encountered stormy weather and heavy traffic at times. One day we shared a small shelter along the Withlacoochie Trail with a local man and his three children, who were out for a family bike outing. With loud thunder claps and lightning all around us, we all huddled together and talked about our favorite bike experiences. Eventually the storm passed, and we biked on in our separate directions, changing our planned route based on the young man's suggestions.

Biking through the unknowns was a big part of the adventure.

Rails to Trails

Biking "rails to trails" around the United States is an entirely different kind of adventure. The old railroad tracks have been removed, and paved or crushed stone bike trails have been built where the trains used to run. Many small towns retain their depots, now converted to visitor centers, restrooms, and restaurants catering to bikers. There are thousands of miles of rails to trails in the United States but none in Southwest Florida.

My favorite trail in Wisconsin is the Elroy-to-Sparta trail that passes through several old train tunnels, one of which is more than a mile in length. It is pitch black inside the tunnel. This thirty-two-mile-long trail connects with other trails that extend to La Crosse and beyond.

The rumor is that Wisconsin Governor Tommy Thompson asked the federal government for funds to help build the Elroy-to-Sparta trail. He invited several congressmen to join him in walking through that longest train tunnel with a flashlight. Halfway through the tunnel, Tommy had the flashlight turned off and it was pitch black. Then, on cue, an assistant turned on a tape recording of an oncoming train. It impressed the politicians enough that they went back to Washington and found the necessary funds to build the bike trail.

Michigan has the Hart-to-Montague trail that is a linear state park for its entire twenty-two-mile length. Another excellent trail runs between Kalamazoo and Holland. Michigan is also blessed with great biking areas through national forests and along the Great Lakes.

Indiana has the Cardinal Trail in the Muncie area and the Monon Trail in Indianapolis. Both are popular biking destinations. Fort Wayne is developing an impressive bike trail system that includes rails to trails. Amish Country and Lake Country in Northern Indiana provide options for biking on lightly traveled roads.

Xenia, Ohio, was once a railroad hub. Now the old depot serves as the hub for rails to trails spoking out in all directions. We have enjoyed the Ohio trails many times. Xenia has done an outstanding job of serving as a biking mecca.

My friend Dave and I biked the Silver Comet Trail from Atlanta, Georgia, to Anniston, Alabama, and back. We were both in our seventies at the time, which presented a unique set of challenges. Our four days on the trail were difficult, satisfying, and enjoyable. It was an opportunity for us to reconnect with each other and work as a team.

Jan and I recently biked the one-hundred-and-fifty-mile Great Appalachian Passage bike trail from Pittsburg, Pennsylvania, to Cumberland, Maryland. It was truly the ride of a lifetime, and we plan to go back next summer. Next year I would love to add the 185-mile C & O Canal Towpath, which extends the trip from Pittsburg all the way to Washington, DC.

Central Florida has beautiful rails to trails. My favorite is the Withlacoochie Trail, which runs for forty-six miles and passes through Floral City, Inverness, and Dunnellon. I've biked this trail at least a dozen times, and it is the trail I prefer to use for my annual "bike my age" ride. Last year it was a seventy-three-mile trek through nature preserves, past large lakes, and through cattle ranches and farmland. In the early morning, squirrels and rabbits outnumbered people on the path. During the five hours it took me to bike my age, there were more bikers on recumbent bikes or trikes than there were on traditional bikes.

The average age of the bikers on the Withlacoochie is probably close to seventy. According to a local resident, many of these same people fought the building of the trail in the late 'eighties, a classic NIMBY (not in my backyard) reaction. Ironically, they are now the beneficiaries of the trail they once opposed.

Biking my age one day each year feels like a booster shot that ensures another year of good health. I hope I can continue to bike my age well into my eighties, and if someone wants to build a rail to trail in Southwest Florida, I promise not to oppose its construction—even if it passes by my backyard.

Potential

When I was in my early thirties, I was a jogger who rarely ran more than a mile or two at a time. I worked with a fellow attorney who trained for and then ran a marathon of twenty-six-plus miles. That was an eye-opener for me, expanding my vision of what was possible. Before I knew it, I was running long distances and competing in 10Ks and 15Ks and even completed the Fort Wayne Marathon. If it had not been for my friend, I probably would have never used those extra gears, and it changed how I viewed my potential.

I was able to carry that simple lesson over from jogging to biking, and we began to move from neighborhood bike rides to rails to trails, bike camping, and eventually to living on our bikes as we toured Germany. All it took was a willingness to use all our gears.

Were it not for these experiences, I doubt I ever would have gathered the courage to leave an established law practice to venture out on my own. I probably would have been stuck and miserable for the rest of my legal career. Instead, I was able to create my own law practice in my own image.

I decided how I wanted to treat my clients and employees. My goal was to be of service, to be helpful, to be kind, and to charge reasonable fees for my services.

I was also fortunate to hire a young woman attorney who had become dissatisfied with the traditional practice of law, and together we formed a team that provided the legal services our clients wanted and deserved. Tracy took over the practice when I retired and has done me proud by growing and improving legal services to our clients over the past fifteen years.

Living in the Process

It is not a bad thing to have goals, whether in life or in biking. Goals give us a much-needed sense of direction. Unfortunately, there can be a tendency to focus on goals to the exclusion of the everyday process of living. When goals or results become our primary focus, we miss out on the experience of life.

I begin each year with the simple goal to bike more than six thousand miles. With that goal out there, I focus on a full appreciation of the joy of each day's ride. Biking can be hypnotic with the repetitive pedaling involved and the rhythm of the ride. Some people refer to biking as a positive addiction. Frequently I experience a feeling akin to a runner's high that is both stimulating and peaceful. And yes, it is addictive—in a good way.

Biking has taught me the value of being in the present moment, fully experiencing the joy and freedom of propelling myself along a path to nowhere. Often I take rest stops in parks or along the beach overlooking the gulf. My route is rarely planned in advance, although I have favorite stops, such as the Naples Pier, Lowdermilk Park, Lely Barefoot Beach, Bonita Beach, Estero Community Park, Three Oaks Park, and the North Collier Water Park. If it were not for biking, I doubt I would be familiar with some of these local treasures of nature. I enjoy the curiosity of people at rest stops who ask about my bike or about my ride.

People often ask me how I can bike in the summer heat of Florida. Ironically, it is my favorite season to bike. Traffic is much lighter in the summer, and moving along at a twelve- to fifteen-mile-per-hour pace creates a breeze that is cooling and refreshing. When the ride is over, I usually jump in the pool.

When we head north to Indiana in June, we take our bikes along. However, riding conditions in the Midwest do not compare to the smooth, flat, designated bike paths of Florida.

Just Do It

Nike has a slogan for their athletic products: "Just do it!" Marathon runners, long-distance bikers, and most other successful athletes have something in common. They do more than just dream about doing it. They actually get out of bed each day and take that first step to train to reach their goals. Thinking about it is the seed. Unless we are willing to actually do it day after day, the thought remains an un-ripened seed or wishful thinking. The secret to success is in the process, not the result.

Road Rage

A small minority of motorists resent sharing the roads with bicyclists. On rare occasions I am squeezed to the edge of the road or yelled at or the subject of a loud, blaring horn. I used to get upset when this happened and reacted with a one-finger salute. Gradually, I've learned that I'm not the person with the problem in those circumstances, and I feel sorry for the motorist who is so angry that he or she would take out his anger on a total stranger. He or she must be having a bad day—or a bad life. Such folks are to be pitied rather than resented.

Ultimately it takes two to have a conflict. If I am unwilling to react to an angry motorist's need to bully, the bullying behavior goes nowhere and my inner peace remains intact.

Recently I had an experience with a commercial truck driver who was providing food services to restaurants and country clubs. The driver must have made a wrong turn, because he was attempting to make a U-turn on a narrow street along the beach. As I approached the truck that was now parked in the bike lane, I went around him. As I passed, the driver blasted his truck horn. I continued and was crossing a bridge when the same truck sped by me with his horn blasting and his right-side mirror about six inches from my left elbow.

I simply memorized the number on the back of the truck and wrote a letter to the company's human resources department describing the situation. I suggested anger-management training for the driver. A week later, I got a phone call apology from the company indicating the driver admitted his behavior and said he was "having a bad day." As a condition of his continued employment, he was required to attend anger-management classes. I got my message across, and he got the help he needed.

Careless Driving

Motorists are becoming more and more aware of bicycles sharing the road, especially in Florida, where bikers sometimes outnumber motorists. Still, it is absolutely necessary for a biker to ride defensively. We are not as visible or obvious as other vehicles, and sometimes drivers are not expecting us to be where we are (e.g., on a sidewalk or path that passes an entrance or exit to a shopping center). In most places, it is legal and acceptable to bike on the sidewalk, always yielding, of course, to any pedestrians who may be sharing the sidewalk. I have learned that it is better to be defensive than to be dead right.

Cell phones are a modern miracle, and I don't know what I would do without my i-phone. However, I do not bike and use my phone at the same time. I find a quiet spot to stop and answer or make a call or to check texts and e-mails. Seeing a biker on the phone makes me cringe. I can spot a car driver on a cell phone a block away and know that I need to be alert and prepared to take evasive action. Texting, of course, is even more of a hazard.

When confronted by a negligent motorist, I have a choice how to react. I can become indignant and angry and completely ruin my own day; or I can let the motorist know in a kind way that he or she just had a near-miss. Without anger, I can tell a motorist that it can be dangerous to cross a sidewalk without looking both ways for bikers and pedestrians. This may raise safety awareness and save another biker on a future ride. No one wants to be responsible for injuring or killing a cyclist or pedestrian, and most people are accepting of the message.

The more I bike, the more careful I become while driving a car. I am much more aware of the danger spots in traffic and have learned to be on the alert for bicyclists and pedestrians who can appear out of nowhere.

Willingness to Be Vulnerable

I often hear people say, "I would never bike alongside car traffic" or "It isn't safe to bike outside the neighborhood." They may be correct in their assessment of the dangers, but sometimes we just need to trust that motorists will be responsible. It is the same trust that we have when we drive a car on a two-lane road. We trust that oncoming cars will remain in their proper lane and not crash head on into our car. Without that degree of trust, we would never venture out into the world.

It can be scary to be biking in a designated bike lane alongside a busy street while seeing dump trucks bearing down in the rearview mirror. Without a reasonable degree of trust, life would be extremely limiting. Biking can be the source of developing that trust.

Common sense can go a long way in keeping a bicyclist safe. Bright, easy-to-spot clothing, flashing lights on the front and rear of the bike, having rear-view mirrors, and wearing a helmet ought to be standard practices. In addition, some discretion can be useful. For example, during snowbird season in Florida I tend to avoid bike lanes on busy streets with high speed limits for motor vehicles. Usually a sidewalk runs alongside the busy street and may be a preferable option to the bike lane at high-traffic times.

Determination

One of the most important lessons any participant sport can teach us is how to be mentally tough. We cannot excel at anything without determination and mental toughness, whether it is baseball, basketball, football, soccer, gymnastics, tennis, golf, wrestling, running, swimming, or biking. They teach us to be disciplined, courageous, and steadfast. This may be why many parents encourage their children to participate in sports. It teaches them important attributes that can help them to excel in life.

It may require effort, dedication, and determination just to get out of bed and onto the bike. Even after we overcome this initial hurdle, it is easy to quit whatever we are doing when we get tired or it becomes difficult. One of the "mind tricks" learned by runners and bikers is to avoid going in circles near home. It is too easy to quit.

The trick on a fifty-mile bike ride is to go twenty-five miles away from home, so there is no choice involved in persevering the entire fifty miles. Personally, I check the wind direction and head into the wind for the first leg, hoping the wind doesn't shift and I can head for home with a tailwind. I may be determined, but I'm not stupid.

All Shapes and Sizes

In Florida we see many young, athletic bikers on racing bikes moving along at a twenty mph clip on a sixty or hundred mile trek. It is easy to admire these athletes. However, the cyclists I most admire and respect are the men and women in their sixties, seventies, or eighties who are using the bike to stay physically and mentally fit. This requires determination, dedication, and motivation.

Southwest Florida's bike paths are full of these bikers—perhaps a testament to the type of people we attract to our area. Many of them were highly successful professionals and community leaders during their younger years and are simply bringing their energetic lifestyles with them into retirement.

For many of the Hispanic workers in our area, a bike is the primary means of transportation. Many of them cannot afford to own a car. When I ride through downtown Bonita Springs, I see as many bikes as motor vehicles. The bikes are often equipped with large baskets for carrying groceries or work tools. The bike provides them with the freedom to get to work, or to the grocery store.

CHAPTER 6

The Practice of Law

Doing Good; then Doing Well

What if being in business
is perceived as a chance to do good?
To assist those in need
without one ounce of greed,
and to do the right thing as we should?
Jb

The American capitalistic system has spawned a great variety of business ventures. We are populated by manufacturers, distributors, builders, tradesmen, suppliers, professionals, entertainers, restaurants, technology companies, utilities, drug stores, grocery stores, service industries, sales and marketing, banking, insurance, mining, farming, recycling, travel, advertising, news media, hospitals, and on and on without limit. There are literally millions of ways to make a living in America.

The practice of law is a unique form of business, in that it can also have an impact on other forms of business. It is a business unto itself and also represents other businesses as well. I was fortunate to have business clients as an important aspect of my law practice.

Not all organizations follow the same business model. Just like individual people, businesses take on characteristics and values (a culture) that makes them unique.

We all know business organizations and professionals whose sole mission is to make a pile of money. A loan shark, a slum landlord, a drug dealer, or an unscrupulous attorney might be extreme examples of this business model, providing dismal service and cutting corners while abusing their customers/clients/suppliers. Typically this kind of business entity will experience a high turnover of disgruntled employees and dissatisfied customers and a reputation that ultimately causes the business or practice to tank. Some of these "business people" spend time in the prison system. Some find their way into politics.

We also know individuals and business organizations whose mission involves doing good. This business model provides extraordinary service to its clients and customers, provides appropriate employee benefits, treats its employees fairly and with respect, exudes integrity, and in the long run often makes a pile of money. It starts out doing good and ends up doing well.

I observed a wide variety of attorneys during my thirty-five years in the business. Most of them were fair, honest, competent, trustworthy, and focused on being helpful. These attorneys reminded me that the practice of law is an honorable profession.

A few attorneys I dealt with were unethical and dishonest, and cared little for the welfare of their clients. For example, there were divorce attorneys who threw gasoline on the fire to create bigger problems and therefore bigger fees. Some attorneys would intentionally prolong legal projects to make the job seem bigger than it was, and lie to their clients or blame others for their misdeeds. For these few, there was a very fine line between being the attorney and being the criminal. Bar associations have not always been successful in weeding these undesirable characters out of the profession.

I never had any doubts about on which side of the fence I intended to practice law.

The practice of law also allowed me to represent many small businesses and counsel them on legal and ethical aspects of doing business. I had an inside look at the ingredients for what I considered genuine success.

An Abundance Mentality

My first experience with the business world occurred before I was ten years old and long before I ventured into the practice of law. It involved the Boeglin Lumber Company, a small operation owned by my dad. At its peak, he employed about forty local men in our hometown of Ferdinand, Indiana. The saw mill supplied wood products for furniture factories in Ferdinand and neighboring towns. One of the byproducts of the business was firewood. As the logs were sawn into lumber, small pieces of scrap wood were discarded onto a pile.

In the 'forties and 'fifties, our small, rural town included some senior citizens who still relied on pot-bellied stoves for heating their homes and cooking their meals. Firewood was an important source of fuel for many of these elderly, poor people. Although the saw mill could have sold the firewood, dad saw the situation differently. He not only made the wood available for free to these folks, but he had my brother Tom, and me, deliver the wood with instructions to sort and stack it neatly for them. We were not allowed to accept any payment for the wood or for our labor. We were sharing in our abundance.

This was a lesson I took with me into the practice of law. Tom incorporated this lesson into his own business as a jeweler and watchmaker, and successfully passed it down to his six children, Debbie, Rick, Tim, Sue, Brian, and Jenny.

Another early lesson learned at The Boeglin Lumber Company was to be responsible for the environment. One of my earliest memories involved planting trees on a 180 acre plot of timberland that had been cut for timber the previous year. For every tree cut down, more trees were planted.

When I was a teenager, it appeared that everyone in town knew dad was dying of cancer. I remember being stopped on my paper route, as my customers would relate stories of what a "great man" my dad was. He died of colon cancer at age 59, with only a modest estate, but he was clearly a rich man who had shared his abundance with the community. He never talked about his acts of kindness. It was only after his death that people told our family about his generosity over the years. He gave freely and quietly, not wanting recognition for his gifts.

Spiritual Awareness

The founder of Sweetwater Sound, Charles, began his business in the 'seventies with a VW Bus that included state-of-the-art (at the time) sound equipment. He traveled to musicians' homes in Northeastern Indiana to become their "sound studio" for recording their music. He helped many fledgling musicians to express their musical talents. Eventually, his reputation spread and he opened up a more elaborate studio in his home. Investing in early computer technology, he became known for his skill and imagination and he was able to help some famous musicians in California to learn to use the new technology more effectively to enhance their music. His focus was always to help others.

Today he employs over 800 people world-wide in the sale and distribution of musical products, and provides sound studios that compete with the world's best. He started out providing outstanding service to his local customers, and he ended up being successful beyond his wildest dreams. I would have loved to have been his legal counsel.

Attention to Detail

Some businesses pay close attention to the bottom line, but overlook attention to providing an extraordinary service. Their focus is backwards. Not so with Wayne, the owner of a travel and conference planning company. The entire focus was on taking care of the customer, trusting that outstanding service would eventually result in a healthy bottom line.

Early in my law practice I had the privilege of representing

Wayne, who had been in charge of convention planning and travel arrangements for a very large insurance company. The insurance company made the decision to sell the travel division, and my client was the obvious buyer. Wayne would continue to handle conferences and travel with the insurance company as his biggest client, while expanding to provide similar services to other companies as well. He was able to take an experienced staff with him in his new venture, and together they continued the attention to detail they had provided for so many years as a division of the insurance company.

Over the years this client, through hard work and dedication to service, built a business that included loyal employees, an outstanding reputation, and successful locations around the State of Indiana. His focus on going the extra mile for his customers translated into happy employees and a successful business. I am thankful for having represented him and his business for over twenty years.

Overcoming Obstacles:

The Erich of E & R Tool scaled the Berlin Wall in order to escape communist opression and, with the help of a sponsoring church, found his way to Indiana to work at his tool and die trade. He and his family became American citizens. Erich worked long and hard at his trade, and eventually teamed up with Robert (the R of E & R) to create the best tool and die shop in the area. They developed skilled, long-term employees and gained a reputation as the "go to" place in Northern Indiana. They did excellent work at a fair price.

Ironically, when nearing retirement, Erich and Robert sold the business to a German company who had a similar reputation. They were able to enjoy the financial benefits of many years of hard work, while providing an ongoing positive work environment for their employees, and excellent service to their customers.

Giving and Receiving:

As a civil engineer, Ron had a vision for helping communities to become better places to live. His focus was on helping rather than on making a pile of money. His company developed a reputation for its creativity and dedication to service. Many small communities in Indiana are now enjoying the benefits of his "gifts."

I first met Ron when we served together on the Unity church board. His generosity toward the church and other charitable organizations was an inspiration for me. He reminded me of my dad, but on a larger stage. His attitude was simple: the more we give, the more we receive.

With a competent and loyal staff in place, Ron was able to transition ownership of his company to his employees. In his retirement years, Ron continues to serve on boards and support charitable causes.

Community Involvement:

Kidd & Company was a family business that spanned a century. As a marshmallow manufacturer in a small Indiana town, it was a major employer and created long-term jobs for generations of employees. The company provided its employees with health insurance benefits long before the requirements of the Affordable

Care Act. An Employee Stock Ownership plan (ESOP) gave employees an ownership opportunity. It seemed like everyone in town wanted to work in this family atmosphere.

Each summer the town celebrated Marshmallow Days, with parades, concessions, rides, and entertainment. Marshmallow Days attracted visitors to the community from far and wide.

When an explosion at a neighboring plant destroyed the company's manufacturing facility in Nevada, they kept their staff intact, putting them to work on community projects such as rehabilitating older homes while the plant was rebuilt. When they were finally able to go back into production, they had an experienced team ready to go back to work.

Doing the Right Thing

Jan and I spent almost ten years with a large, powerful national real estate broker. Over time we noticed that their corporate focus seemed to shift away from service to their bottom line, with little care about the success of their real estate agents who generated their sales or the customers they represented.

When our much-loved local broker needed time off to be with her husband who was dying of cancer, the company replaced her because her husband "took too long to die." It was at this point that Jan and I, along with other top producers in the office, decided it was time to move on.

Our broker subsequently joined a small, regional real estate firm, where she now manages almost all the top realtors who had previously been with the gigantic firm. Roughly $100,000,000 in annual real estate sales have been lost to the old firm due to its failure to do the right thing.

The focus of our new brokerage firm is to provide outstanding service to its customers and to help its agents to be successful. The owners understand that if their customers are happy and their agents are successful, the company will also prosper. Working with the new firm has been a pleasure and a privilege.

Service

Southwest Florida is blessed with many successful retirees who continue to give of their talents in their retirement years. Our community is the beneficiary of their gifts, and the givers benefit from the satisfaction of doing something worthwhile even in their retirement years.

I have a couple of golf buddies who were builders during their working careers—Terry built houses in Pennsylvania; George built churches throughout the Midwest. Together, they volunteer one day per week building homes through Habitat for Humanity. Their skills and experience are invaluable in the building of these homes. Their service is priceless in enriching their own retirement years.

Many former business executives and professionals populate the boards of local churches, hospitals, and charitable organizations. They are giving of their time, talents, and money to make our community a better place for everyone.

Retired teachers freely offer their services as tutors for struggling students, or teach English as a second language to immigrants and their children. These teachers gain as much benefit from their service as do their students.

Jan has a background as Beedeedle the Clown. Several years ago, she, along with her cohort Pipsqueak, established and trained a "clowns on rounds" group at Naples Community Hospital. She continues to take time out of her busy real estate schedule to entertain and uplift patients and staff at the hospital. It is easy for me to see that she is the primary beneficiary of her efforts. She returns home happier and more energized than when she left.

Our friend Linda volunteers her time on a weekly basis to work at the food pantry operated by Bonita Springs Assistance Office. She, along with a group of volunteers, is instrumental in providing much-needed food, diapers, and other vital supplies to the poorest residents of Bonita Springs. The joy and personal satisfaction she receives far exceeds the effort she puts into this worthwhile work.

Dave and Sandy use their retirement years to make a difference in their church, helping it to become an environmentally friendly, open and welcoming congregation. They are also active in an organization promoting peace in the Middle East—not an easy challenge. Dave continues to mentor counseling students as they prepare to enter the challenging world of mental health therapy. Dave and Sandy are role models for successful retirement.

CHAPTER 7

The Inevitable Process of Aging

Lessons Learned from Our Elders

What if, as the German expression says,
we get too soon old and too late smart?
What if, as the saying goes,
it's never too late for a fresh start?

As far as we know, we have a one-way ticket
To a destination shrouded in mystery.
As we travel, it's up to each one of us
To write and create our own history!
Jb

Sunsets

Those of us who live on the west coast of Florida are familiar with sunsets. People gather on the beach in the evenings to cheer that great ball of fire as it meets its watery grave out in the gulf. Sunsets in this part of the world can be awe-inspiring.

Florida is also home to many folks who are in the sunset years of their lives. These years can be awe-inspiring, or they can be filled with pain, illness, hardships, loneliness, and depression.

It is widely believed that our thoughts have a major impact on our circumstances. I have spent a large part of my life around older people, and I see a lot of truth in this observation. Our thoughts do have a tremendous impact on the quality of our lives.

As the youngest of seven children, born to parents in their mid-forties, I was surrounded by elderly aunts and uncles. My grandmother came to live with us when she was in her mid-eighties and died in our home at age eighty-nine. I was thirteen at the time of her death in 1956. She was a significant influence in my life, freely sharing her thoughts and philosophies with me. Grandma Remke was calm, peaceful, and softly mellowed. She not only raised a large family under difficult conditions, but she lovingly contributed her talents and abilities to our family until the very end.

In 1956 there were no automatic dishwashers in Ferdinand. Dishes were washed by hand, and it was Grandma's job to wash the supper dishes while I dried them and put them away. We worked as a team. There came a time when she could no longer wash the supper dishes. When she could no longer contribute to the family unit, she decided it was time to go. She retired to her room and died within a matter of days.

A Sickly Child

My mother, Clara, took after her own mother. A sickly child, she was not expected to live to adulthood. Nonetheless, she had the mental toughness to overcome her sickliness, and she gave birth to, and raised, seven children—her first child was born when she was twenty-eight and the seventh at age forty-six. In her later years, she substituted common sense for the religious and societal dogma she had been fed most of her life. She became an independent thinker and loved to talk politics. She liked President Kennedy even more than she liked the pope.

Although she owned a car, Clara walked everywhere, declining rides from well-meaning friends and relatives. She loved to exercise. I remember calling her on her eighty-fifth birthday, a Saturday in early October, and asking her what she was doing to celebrate her birthday. It turns out she was watching the World Series on television, listening to the Indiana University football game on the radio, and exercising on her stationary bicycle—all at the same time! Knowing her, she was also praying the rosary and asking for an IU victory.

Mom lived independently until age ninety-two and died just a week short of her ninety-fourth birthday. She was a widow for thirty-two years. In all the years I knew her, I never heard her complain. According to my sister Ann, who was a hospice nurse and took Mother into her home for her final two years, Clara was a delight to the very end.

Elder Law Practice

Much of my thirty-five years as an attorney were spent developing a law practice in Fort Wayne, Indiana, that included elder law issues.

Most of these clients were over sixty, and some of them were over ninety. Many of them were happy, funny, active contributors to the community. They were veritable fountains of wisdom and knowledge. I enjoyed their company, and I probably learned as much from them as they did from me.

From my clients I learned that attitude was an important element of their aging process. I had clients who, in their sixties, wanted my help in finding appropriate assisted living arrangements. Often these clients didn't live long enough to need the assistance. They had unknowingly allowed an old person to creep into their minds and hearts. Their thoughts and fears were all about the infirmities of old age, and they stopped living in the present moment.

Then I remember Frank, a client who was eighty-nine years old and living alone since the recent death of his wife. He had an eighty-five-year-old sister who was legally blind but also lived independently. One Friday afternoon after his appointment with me about a tax matter, I asked him about his plans for the weekend. He informed me that he was driving his blind sister to Columbus, Ohio, to visit an older sister—who also lived independently in her own home. This was a trip of about one hundred and sixty miles in each direction, and he never doubted that he was capable of making the trip successfully. At age eighty-nine, he did not think of himself as an old person.

Florida Real Estate

Shortly after my heart bypass surgery in 2001, I transferred the law practice to my younger partner, Tracy. I became "of counsel," and Jan and I retired to Florida. We determined very quickly that retirement was not for us—at least not at that stage of our lives. We became licensed Florida Realtors and formed the Boeglin Team, for the first ten years with a large national firm in Bonita Springs, and more recently with Royal Shell Real Estate in Naples. Our clientele is often in their sixties, seventies, or eighties.

Similar to my experience in the law practice, we find that being realtors is all about serving the clients' needs. We have developed an awareness of the needs of older clients, and we know we serve them well. We also enjoy getting to know clients as they pass through a very significant step in their lives—whether it involves buying their dream home in Florida, downsizing or upsizing to a different home, or selling their home due to the illness or death of a spouse, or making the difficult decision to move to assisted living. Every situation is a learning experience.

Different clients handle these milestones in different ways. For some, the stress overpowers their inner peace; others successfully manage their emotions and attitudes and go with the flow of the transaction. Jan and I have learned not to judge another person's process and to be non-defensive and understanding when an overstressed person acts out of fear. Sometimes fears need to be acknowledged before they can be released.

A Common Denominator

If there is one common denominator for all of humankind, it is that we all begin the aging process the day we are born and continue to age every day of our lives. Aging is not a positive or a negative concept. It is simply a fact of life. Each one of us, consciously or unconsciously, decides what the experience is for ourselves.

In the early parts of our lives, we are growing, strengthening, developing our talents, and learning as we "grow up." If we are fortunate to live long enough, at some point the aging process changes direction and we begin to lose physical strength, endurance, athletic ability, hearing, sight, and mental quickness. It is at this stage that our thoughts, attitudes, and emotions determine if we become fearful, depressed, mean, and cranky old people or if we welcome this special and inevitable chapter of our lives. We have a choice: we can pass through our golden years kicking and screaming, or we can accept our circumstances and become calm, peaceful, and softly mellowed.

I do not consider acceptance of aging as a sign of weakness. It takes a strong person to accept reality and learn to adapt to changes. I would argue that non-acceptance may be the sign of weakness. Making the best of the situation requires flexibility, determination, and strength of character.

Interestingly, we did not all grow up at the same pace, and we do not proceed at the same pace in the latter stages of our lives. Chronologically, of course, we pass our years together. Our birthdays occur roughly every 365 days. However, the choices we make in our early years can impact the pace and quality of our aging later on. And it is never too late to make better choices for ourselves—choices like an exercise program or healthier diet, stopping smoking, learning yoga, or developing inner peace.

Generally, people who live healthy, active lifestyles age more gracefully than people who have been "couch potatoes," abuse alcohol, tobacco, or drugs, or follow an unhealthy diet. How well we learn to deal with stress can also be an important determining factor for how well we age.

From my experience, accepting the aging process does not mean that we become calm, peaceful lumps. Many of the so-called elderly continue to live meaningful, productive, happy lives until the very end. In Florida, I see people in their eighties and nineties walking, swimming, biking, playing tennis, golfing, working out, and maintaining their physical and mental health to a ripe old age. Many of them volunteer their services to charitable organizations that desperately need their talents and remain involved and engaged in life.

They (we) hold the wisdom of the ages, and it is important to share our life experiences with younger generations. Some of us may not be technically savvy, but we may have a perspective on issues that is helpful to younger folks. We can be a stabilizing influence in an unstable world. We have a longer view of the world and its challenges than do subsequent generations.

Because I intend to be one of those calm, peaceful, and softly mellowed persons as I (hopefully) move through my seventies and beyond, I have paid careful attention to my role models. From my grandmother and mother, to my elder law clients, to our real estate clients and friends, I have observed, asked questions, and been acutely aware of the people I intend to emulate.

This chapter is about what I see as some of the keys that make for a happy, healthy, active, and productive time of life. Here's to happy and healthy golden years!

Having a Sense of Purpose

The need to empty a bladder might get us out of bed in the morning, but it is not reason enough to enjoy a new day. I believe none of us is here just to take up space on the planet. People who succeed in life have a sense of purpose—whether they are a twenty-year-old student, a forty-year-old professional, or an eighty-year-old retiree.

Purpose can take many forms. For some of us, it is spiritual or religious in nature; others find purpose in the physical world of business, politics, teaching, helping others, volunteering, sports, fitness, family, friends, hobbies, or relationships. Purpose almost always involves serving, contributing, and giving. Fulfillment comes from giving, not getting. The most miserable people I know are takers. The happiest people I know are givers—of their energy, talents, kindnesses, and/or money—to help others.

Living on purpose cures a lot of life's problems. It means constructing a way of living that is in harmony with our purpose. It means choosing thoughts, forming habits, and developing attitudes that are aligned with our purpose. It means finding ways to be useful, helpful contributors to the common welfare of our community and our world.

Some people have a clear vision of their mission here and live it out day after day. Others sometimes search to find meaning and purpose in their daily lives. Drifting through life without a sense of purpose can lead to depression, sadness, and lack of energy or motivation. Whenever I sense that I am "adrift," I go inside and remember why I am here and how I can make a positive difference in my world. Writing down a plan of action can be an effective way to recover my sense of purpose.

Creating Structure

Most of us had structure in our lives during the years we were in school, employed, and/or raising a family. We had daily schedules, goals, activities, deadlines, events, and responsibilities. We did not drift through those years without any idea how we were going to use our time. The external requirements led us through our busy lives.

Retirement removes some of the external structures of our former lives, and it is up to us to create new internal systems to avoid drifting aimlessly through our retirement years. This is a time when we have an opportunity to develop our own life structure, rather than having structure imposed upon us by a teacher, an employer, or family obligations. Granted, it might be a more relaxed, less demanding way of living in retirement. There is a fine line between having constant demands on our time, and enjoying projects, being productive, and feeling useful.

Personally, I like to plan ahead in my Franklin Covey Planner. I schedule activities in advance, knowing when I intend to be golfing, biking, writing, working, socializing, doing chores, etc. It isn't unusual for plans to change as unexpected opportunities or obstacles arise. Structure does not need to be set in concrete. I find that I am more productive and a happier person when I have a plan. My slow days are when I feel adrift.

Different people create structure in different ways. For some, it may mean meeting a group of friends every morning for breakfast and telling stories; regularly scheduled bridge, gin, or mahjong games can provide this structure; working out at the gym on a set schedule can fill the need for structure; many retirees I know spend a day or more per week volunteering at a hospital or church, connecting with fellow volunteers; regular involvement with a service club such as The Rotary can provide needed structure; and morning bike rides or walks, alone or with friends, can be a consistent form of structure. The nature of the structure may be less important than the presence of structure in our lives.

A Supportive Environment

As we age, there can be a tendency to become negative. I sometimes hear folks bemoaning how bad things are: in our country, in our community, with the younger generation, regarding their health, losing friends and family members to illness and death, politicians, corruption, terrorism, traffic, taxes, neighbors, changing societal trends, etc.

I am not advocating that we bury our heads in the sand and ignore societal issues. Things are not perfect, nor have they ever been. Life is a work in process, and we are all a piece of the puzzle. We have a choice of whether to drag our world down or lift it up. Being negative does not solve problems; it accentuates them.

There have been times in my life when I have lived in the midst of anger and negativity. I have learned to make a conscious effort to move away from such situations and to find people and circumstances that resonate with positive energy. Whiners and complainers do nothing for me except remind me it is not how I choose to live my life. I can't change other people's attitudes, but I can model a different way to be. Sometimes that is all it takes.

Sometimes modeling positive behavior can make a difference but not always. Some people love to wallow in misery. I have been fortunate to find many friends who are upbeat, positive, energetic, and generally happy. These folks enjoy their friends' successes rather than being envious. They are aware and appreciate the efforts to be helpful and are grateful for their family and friends. They don't judge or condemn each other; they understand and support one another. In the process, everyone in the group is lifted up rather than torn down.

Open Mindedness

You would think that the longer we have lived, and the more life experiences we have had, we would naturally become more open minded as we age. That isn't always the case. There can be a tendency to retrench, become more rigid in our beliefs, and think our approach is the only approach.

I prefer to associate with people who are tolerant of people who are different than themselves, whether the difference is age, race, gender, religious beliefs, or economic circumstances. These folks are somehow able to look beyond the form and focus on the content that is the underlying spirit of the person.

My mother, Clara, was an example for me. She shed much of the religious dogma that had been thrust upon her for decades. She widened her worldview and became more tolerant and less judgmental of others as she aged. I see this characteristic being emulated in my siblings and in the next generation of Boeglins. My goal is to follow in her footsteps.

CHAPTER 8

Finishing Strong

Thoughts for the Final Leg of the Journey

What if we worry and obsess
about things beyond our control?
Does living in fear solve the mess
or unduly torture the soul?
jb

Where does life go from here?

Before we know it, we are heading into the home stretch of our lives. For me, nearly three-quarters of a century has passed in the blink of an eye. I can look in the rearview mirror and see a much longer path behind me than what remains before me. I have been blessed with opportunities to learn from great teachers who have shared my path. Sometimes I have paid attention; sometimes I have fallen asleep in class.

My teachers have included grandparents, parents, siblings, wives, children, grandchildren, uncles and aunts, nieces and nephews, friends, priests, nuns, ministers, politicians, professors, authors, fellow board members, therapists, law partners, golf buddies, bike companions, clients, attorneys, sales clerks, servers, and even perfect strangers.

I ask myself questions like: How do I want to experience whatever is left of this final leg of the journey? What do I still need to learn? What can I share with my fellow travelers? How can I live fully and deeply as I age?

A recent phone call put life into perspective for me. I was biking in Naples when I received a phone call from my nephew, Tim. When I saw that the call was from Bloomington, Indiana, I stopped my bike and answered my phone. He asked me what I was doing, and I told him I was biking. That was his dream as well. Unfortunately, Tim was calling to thank me for being his uncle and an inspiration for him, and to say good-bye. It was one of the saddest, and most meaningful, phone calls I have ever received. It was hard to bike my way home with tears in my eyes.

Tim was diagnosed with a rare form of cancer at age fifty-five. In an effort to prolong his life, his left leg was amputated above the knee. Tim went on with his brilliant life. He golfed and biked with a prosthetic leg. Always a person with big ideas, he and his wife, Cindy, decided to take Tim's octogenarian parents on a walking tour of Italy. Less than a year before his death, and with only one leg, Tim led Cindy, their son Gus, and Tom and Betty as they walked their way around Italy's attractions. Tim never tired and never complained.

Tim's sister, Sue, was Indiana's lieutenant governor at the time of his leg amputation. Tim had been one of Sue's strongest campaign supporters when she was elected to office. Rather than feeling sorry for himself, he told Sue, "Now I can better stump for you." He maintained his sense of humor and love of others until he drew his last breath.

A graduate of Notre Dame and the Indiana University School of Law, Tim was a successful entrepreneur and teacher. He was also a strong family man, actively involved with Cindy in raising two sons. He maintained close relationships with his five siblings and his parents. Tim was loved by his family and friends.

On the day that he had decided to stop the last of a long series of experimental treatments, he did not crawl under a rock to die. Somehow, Tim mustered the courage and the energy to call several important people in his life, to thank them, and to say good-bye. That is my definition of finishing strong.

Acceptance

We must learn to accept things we cannot change: "God, grant me the serenity to accept the things I cannot change, the courage to change the things I can, and the wisdom to know the difference." This is the Serenity Prayer.

Tim battled cancer with every ounce of his energy. His life was prolonged, and probably in some ways enhanced, by his difficult experience. He did what he could to alter the course of this dreaded disease, and in the end he accepted the reality of the situation. He accepted what he could not change but did what he could to live fully to the very end.

We live on a fragile planet that is constantly changing. The inhabitants of the planet don't always behave according to our standards or expectations. If we spend our lives obsessing about events beyond our control, we are wasting our brief time on earth. S*** happens!

That is not to say that we ought not to care about disease, famines, earthquakes, tsunamis, typhoons, hurricanes, wildfires, floods, droughts, plagues, terrorist actions, violent crime, mass shootings, poverty, drunk drivers, corrupt or deranged politicians, religious wars, foreign dictators, ecological disasters, economic depressions, etc. It is a noble endeavor to help the victims and to work to minimize the damage. We may even become involved in groups focused on promoting peace, rescuing refugees, spreading medical technology to poor countries, voting the crooks out of office, fostering religious or racial tolerance, or reversing manmade climate change.

Some things are beyond our control, but we can take steps to protect ourselves from disaster. The stock market is an example. It seems to have a life of its own, dictated by forces beyond my control. However, I can invest my nest egg in ways that alleviate the major risks of market fluctuations. Likewise, the housing market will follow its path without input from me. I can, however, make decisions that are appropriate for my circumstances and financial situation. I can be a prudent, responsible investor.

I've noticed over the years that very few people behave based on my expectations of them. Everyone seems to live their lives based on their experiences, their vision, and their needs. What I want them to do is irrelevant.

If I expect a family member or friend to act according to my expectations, I am in for a frustrating life. If I expect my congressman or senator to do the right thing, I may be bitterly disappointed. If a political candidate says things that sound crazy or dangerous to me, I can vote for another candidate—or I can worry myself sick. If I expect my children to parent my grandchildren exactly the way I would do it, relationships with my children will undoubtedly be strained.

Changing the Things I Can

So, what is within my control? My thoughts, feelings, habits, and behavior! My mother always told me, "We are what we eat." I have come to believe we are what we think.

Most people in the Western world are fortunate to live in a free society that, within reason, allows freedom of thought and freedom of expression. Perhaps the most valued freedom I have is the freedom to choose my thoughts. I cannot speak for everyone, but I know my thoughts determine the quality of my life. When I choose fearful, negative, judgmental thoughts, I become an angry, miserable, unhappy person. When I choose positive, happy, accepting thoughts, life is good. The root cause of the quality of my life is thought.

We all know people who have every privilege and advantage and have more talent, money, and property than they know what to do with, yet they are miserable, unhappy whiners. Their thoughts focus on fears, insecurities, greed, and perceived lacks. On the other end of the spectrum, I know people with very little who choose to share what they have, help others, and appreciate their blessings. They choose grateful, positive, loving thoughts, and their lives are enhanced.

The thoughts I choose, more than any other factor, determine the quality of my life. Therefore, it makes sense to me to focus on my thoughts—the thing over which I have the most control. If my life is not proceeding in a satisfactory manner, I can change my thoughts and change my life.

Habits

I believe our daily habits are the result of the thought patterns we choose. Over time, thoughts evolve into habits, and habits are the foundation of the circumstances of our daily lives. If we develop healthy, kind, productive habits, our circumstances follow suit. If we develop selfish, lazy, unhealthy habits, our circumstances in life will eventually reflect those habits.

My thoughts determine the kind of exercise I give to my body on a daily basis. If the weather (which I cannot control) is not conducive to biking, I can choose to walk or work out in the gym. If I choose to do nothing, I can choose to forgive myself and accept a day off from physical exercise. Or I can choose to feel guilty. It's my call.

My thoughts determine the quality and quantity of food I put into my body. My eating habits have a big impact on my health. When I eat healthy, it is because of the thoughts I select. When I eat junk food or drink too much, I have chosen the impact on my body, and I am free to change my thoughts.

Whether I smoke is a personal decision that no one else controls but me. The same goes for addictive drugs or medications. My thoughts determine if I have these habits. No one has the power to take my free thoughts away from me. Addictions present a unique challenge, but ultimately I decide for myself.

The quality of my golf game is largely determined by the thoughts I select on any given day. I can be my own worst enemy, thinking of myself as an incompetent idiot, a born loser; or I can choose to be my own best friend, listening to my inner pro and caddie, who are confident and positive. It is my decision.

My thoughts determine how I treat other people in my life. Do I choose fearful, angry, bigoted, racist thoughts? Do I choose kind, respectful, loving thoughts? Our actions toward others are the direct result of our thoughts, the one thing over which we have absolute control.

The World I See around Me Is a Reflection of What Is Inside of Me

I am learning that I see what I want to see and hear what I want to hear. No matter the circumstance in my life, I look inside first. My internal frame of reference determines what I see outside of me. My thoughts, ideas, and emotions create my reality. I can look around and see my own state of mind.

When I see the world around me going to hell in a hand basket, I can be pretty sure that my inner consciousness is not functioning at a high level. When I am fearfully obsessing and worrying, I know that I am disconnected from my Divine Source. When I am happy and content, I am also feeling the connection.

If I don't like what I see in my external world, I always have the choice to work from the inside out to change my world for the better.

The cost of giving is receiving

There is an old karmic concept: What goes around comes around. We are giving out something all of the time. If we want to know what we are giving out, we only need to look at what we are receiving.

Do we feel that someone is not respecting us? Perhaps a closer look at our own behavior will demonstrate a lack of respect for that person. Do we feel loved and accepted by the people around us? Could it be that we are a loving and accepting person?

My nephew, Tim, treated everyone around him with loving kindness. In return, he was loved and respected by everyone in his life. That was no accident.

Whenever we are unhappy with our life circumstances, we have the power to change our thoughts, attitudes, and behavior. Inevitably, our circumstances will change and align with our new state of consciousness.

It is never wrong to do the right thing

We are the ultimate beneficiaries of our choices. There may be temporary payoffs from failing to do the right thing, but in the long run it is always damaging. Failing to do the right thing adversely affects how we feel about ourselves, which in turn adversely affects the quality of our lives.

Golf is a sport based on integrity, and it is largely self-policing. When a golfer intentionally breaks a rule of golf, it always comes back to bite him. The impact of cheating may not be in the same round, but choosing to dispense with integrity can result in bad golf, loss of reputation, loss of business relationships, and loss of friends.

Failing to do the right thing in business is a recipe for long term disaster. When we treat our employees and customers without service and integrity, we are ultimately penalizing ourselves. Recently one of our sellers called Jan "too honest" because she insisted that he disclose to buyer's realtor a problem with the garage door. For Jan, that was the supreme compliment.

Finding a wallet loaded with cash presents a choice for the finder: he can take the cash and dispose of the wallet; or he can find the owner of the wallet, and return it intact. The decision that is made will have a long term effect on the psyche of the finder. If he keeps the cash, he will probably not feel very good about himself. If he does the right thing, he will forever be a better person for the experience.

Cheating in relationships is the leading cause of nasty and expensive divorces, unhappy family conditions, and more dysfunctional relationships to follow. Short term pleasure inevitably leads to long term pain.

Attack is born out of fear and weakness:

There is a common misperception that when we attack another person, we are exhibiting strength; and when we are defenseless, we are weak. In my opinion, the reverse is true. Only weak people bully or attack other people. Only insecure people belittle other people or call them derogatory names.

I believe people attack because they are afraid. They bully because they feel inadequate. Attacking or ridiculing another person does not require strength. It is a cowardly behavior and a cry for help. A strong person has no need to bully or intimidate.

Being defensive requires no inner strength. When attacked, the knee-jerk reaction is to counterattack, protect, and defend. The more difficult and courageous response is to be defenseless. Conflict cannot flourish when there is a non-defensive reaction. Cross accusations and blame only fuel the fires of battle. Being open to understanding the rationale or cause of the attack can lead to solutions.

For or Against:

Some people tend to focus on the problem; others have learned to focus on the solution. I believe that being **for** a noble cause is more effective that being **against** deviant behavior.

- We can be opposed to violence, whether in the form of violent crime, terrorist activities, war, bullying, or abusive behavior; or we can work to promote peace in every circumstance.
- We can be against bigotry and racism; or we can be for equality of all people everywhere, regardless of religion,

color of skin, sexual orientation, political affiliations, or
economic circumstances.

- We can declare war on poverty; or we can work for shared
  prosperity and economic fairness in government and
  business.
- We can fight against "Extreme Islamic Terrorism"; or we
  can demonstrate religious tolerance and acceptance of
  religious beliefs that may be different than our own.
- We can focus on fear; or we can focus on love.

Golf teaches this concept to me on a regular basis. As I get ready
to hit my second shot on Hole #16 at Estero CC, a difficult dogleg
right over water, I have a choice: I can tell myself: "Don't hit the
ball into the water." Almost always, fear enters my mind. As a
result, I often dump the shot in the lake. On the other hand, I
can tell myself: "Hit the ball onto the green and next to the pin."
Usually, fear is nowhere in my consciousness and I am focused on
hitting the ball onto the green. The results tend to be much more
positive.

Be Prepared; Show Up

One day I was sharing my frustration with an upcoming challenge
in the law practice. My friend gave me advice that I have taken with
me wherever I go, whether I am involved in a business transaction,
a personal issue, my golf game, or a bike adventure. Her formula
was simple and straightforward:

- Be prepared for the challenge. This means doing my
  homework, getting myself physically, mentally, emotionally
  and spiritually ready for the challenge.

- Show up. Don't find an excuse to avoid or delay the challenge.
- Pay attention. Avoid distractions and be totally focused.
- Tell the truth. Have the integrity to do the right thing.
- Don't get attached to a result. Stay in the process. Once our mind jumps to focusing on a desired result, a desirable result becomes elusive.

Applying this formula to the sale of a client's business in the practice of law, I can research all aspects of the law that may come into play in the transaction and share my thoughts with the business owners. Then, we can all show up on time for the negotiation sessions. It is important to pay attention to the body language and the nuances of the parties, to determine motivation and integrity. The details of the transaction will be in the contract and attachments. Misleading or lying to the buyer or the buyer's attorney is not acceptable. Most importantly, don't get attached to the successful sale of the business until the deal is completed. Becoming attached to a result during the process will inevitably weaken bargaining power.

Similarly, in the sale of a home listed by our real estate team, market research must be prepared and shared with the homeowner to prepare the seller for the reality of the market. Once the home is on the market, one of us tries to be available 24/7 in the real estate business, so that we can be there when an offer is forthcoming. Thorough attention to the terms of the offer is critical to a successful real estate transaction, as are suggested counteroffers if appropriate. Assessing the motivation of the buyer can be useful in guiding the seller with respect to responses to an offer. Full disclosure of all relevant information about the history and condition of the home is required, and can avoid litigation after the sale. And remember, there can be obstacles to concluding the sale such as financing contingencies and inspection issues, so it is important not to get attached to a particular deal until after it is closed and the check is cashed.

Now is My Time; Here is My Place

During the 'nineties I helped to found, and then served on the board of The Network for Attitudinal Healing International. NAHI was a network that connected the Centers for Attitudinal Healing in North America, South America, Europe, Africa, and Australia. We provided conferences, trainings, and support.

Dr. Jerry Jampolsky, a Child Psychiatrist in Tiburon, California, was a fellow board member. He created the Principles of Attitudinal Healing in his best-selling book, Love is Letting Go of Fear. That book had been an important resource for helping me through the emotional aspects of the dissolution of my marriage ten years earlier, and I felt privileged to serve along-side Jerry. He was a teacher and mentor for me.

The fifth principle that Dr. Jampolsky shares in his book is: "Now is the only time there is, and each instant is for giving."

Over the years I have evolved my own variation of this Principle in the form of a daily affirmation: Now is the time; this is the place. I am here, now, for a reason. It reminds me to fully appreciate right here, right now. There is no other time or place I would rather be.

As I bike, or write, or golf, or work with clients or other realtors, or socialize with family or friends, this affirmation is now part of my consciousness. The thought deepens the experience, no matter what is happening or where I am. It helps me to be fully present, fully engaged.

Tim Boeglin learned this lesson long before I did.

Every situation in life is a "teaching moment"

Our lives are blessed with teachers who appear to us in a variety of situations and circumstances. Some of our teachers demonstrate how **not** to be. One of the most difficult lessons in life is to also appreciate these teachers, and to forgive them.

My first law partner taught me how **to be,** and also how **not to be.** He taught me a lot about the practice of law, and I will be forever grateful for his mentorship. He was always generous with his time with me, and seemed to enjoy the role of teacher. Eventually, his "inner demons" seemed to overwhelm him and being his partner became uncomfortable for me. It took every ounce of my energy to leave the old law firm on a kind note. Somehow, I pulled it off. In subsequent years, he became an important referral source for my new law practice, and we parted as friends.

Political campaigns provide vast opportunities to observe human behavior, and to understand the role of the ego in this competitive environment. It is tempting for our own egos to join in the political fight. It appears to be human nature to want to be right and to prove "them" wrong.

Family dynamics offer a wonderful laboratory for learning. As we relate to our parents, siblings, spouses, and children, we learn about ourselves. On a daily basis, we are provided with the opportunity to learn and to grow, or to blame and to judge.

Our workplaces involve interactions with fellow human beings, as co-workers, bosses, customers, clients, and competitors. How we interact determines how we feel about ourselves, and how we feel toward other people.

The golf course abounds with teaching moments if we are open to them. Every challenge is also an opportunity to learn and to grow. It is the reason many of us play the game.

Time on the bicycle has been, for me, a time to think about what type of person I intend to be, today and in the future. It provides a peaceful time to be introspective and figure out the paths I intend to take in my remaining time here. At age 74, I still consider the bike to be a most important vehicle for my life's journey.

About the Author

Jim Boeglin has resided in Bonita Springs, Florida since 2001, and has biked every inch of Bonita Springs, Naples, and Estero. He lives with his wife, Jan, and their cats, Charlie and Lizzy. Their home is in Spanish Wells, and they play golf at the nearby Estero Country Club. Together they formed The Boeglin Team in 2003, and later added Jim Griffith and Fred Cuthbertson to the Team. Jan has evolved into the lead Realtor, with Jim as the backup singer.

Daughter Laura Vorderman lives with her husband, Dave, and son, Robbie, on Lake James near Angola, Indiana, where Robbie is a senior in high school and headed for Ball State University. Laura, a former school teacher, and Dave own and operate Vorderman Auto Body in Fort Wayne.

Son Mike is married to Lis, and recently moved from NYC to Seattle. Mike is director of global technology for an NGO, PATH of Seattle. He and Lis have become world travelers.

Daughter Stacey Monnier lives with husband, Tom, and their children, Katelyn, Alex, and Gabby. Stacey has been a CPA with Raytheon since she graduated from IU almost a quarter century ago.

All three children are proud graduates of Indiana University. Go Hoosiers!

Printed in the United States
By Bookmasters